The Virtuous Wife Unveiled

By PJ MCLAUGHLIN

Willow Creek Publishing LLC

Web site: willowcreekpublishingllc.com

e-mail: asher@willowcreekpublishing.com

INDEX

Dedication

I dedicate this book to a former Pastor of mine, Pastor Scott Walsh. When I first joined his church, he had a custom of giving all new members a verse for life. Little did he know at that time what that verse was to become to me. This book and others to come are by products of that calling.

Titus 2:4 & 5. That they may teach the young women to be sober, to love their husbands, to love their children, To be discreet, chaste, keepers at home, good, obedient to their own husbands, that the word of God be not blasphemed.

This book has reformed me, as I hope it does you. It is my belief that we don't always take seriously God's Word. If we don't like what we think He's telling us, we say, "That doesn't apply to me." In our pious spirituality, we become above God's Word. It is time we started taking a closer look at His Word and our attitude.

This book is an attempt to do away with the mistaken belief that it is impossible for one woman to reach the ideal of the Proverbial Virtuous Wife. Not only is she the ideal wife, but what she does is common sense, and very possible for every woman to achieve, even in today's world.

A LITTLE ABOUT THIS BOOK AND THE HANDS GOD USED TO WRITE IT:

If you are looking for a quick read and flattering words, this is not it. But if you truly want to know what Proverbs 31 is saying and how you can become a virtuous wife, read on.

To begin, I believe God should receive all the credit for this book. It is based on His Words not mine. Although, not perfectly written, I hope it is understandable. Remember, God's Words are perfect, but the instrument He used to write this book is not. I pray His words will come through loud and clear and mine will be left on the page unseen.

Much of what is written would lead many to believe that I have my life in complete surrender to the Lord. Unfortunately, this is not the case. I am still struggling with many of the things in this book. Many pastors will tell you their best sermons are the ones they need to hear themselves. That holds true here. This book was written because I needed, still need, the message.

The book is divided into sections:

- The first is a brief breakdown of the verses we will be studying. My subscript on each will give a very brief account of what is in the chapter for that section.
- The prescription gives a starting point and brief outline of how to use this book.
- Each chapter starts with discussion questions that should be answered individually before reading that

chapter. You will need a notebook for this. Start your notes off with your answers and notes from the prescription and word studies in chapter one.

- Appendix I is my answers to the discussion questions. But please, don't cheat. Answer them yourself before checking my answers; you may come up with better ideas than I did.

- Appendix II, Key to other translations & recommended reading.

- The Leader's guide is for those studying the book on their own, or for the leaders of a group, if you want to use the book for a group study. It includes meeting notes, and if reading on your own, should be read before each corresponding chapter.

- And, last you will find my testimony. At least in part.

A Pastor in Kenya gave the following advice to some young ladies in his congregation. It so fit the message of this book I asked him for permission to use it here. I know most of the woman reading this book are already married, but I'm sure you know many who are not, that could benefit from this advice:

Pastor Kipkirui

ADVICE FOR WOMEN IN THE DATING WORLD

You will never convince a man to love you.
Find a man who answers when you call and texts back within minutes rather than days.
Find a man that gives you clear cut answers and doesn't leave you wondering where you stand.
Find a man that wants to make you a part of his life rather than a chapter in his book.
Find a man who doesn't take years and years to figure out what he wants from you.
Find a man who respects, celebrates and encourages your individuality, your education, your spirituality, and your growth.
Remember It is never asking too much from a man to be considered a priority.
Find a man who is genuinely interested in you and pursues you on a daily basis.
Find a man who asks you to go to church with him.
Find a man who prays with you
Find a man that never lets you go to sleep at night wondering if you still matter.

Watch how a man treats his mother. You can learn a lot from how someone treats the person that brought them into this world.

Never chase a man because of his looks because one day those looks will eventually fade and what your left with is what's inside so don't be consumed by his physical traits.

Find a man who protects you and stands up for you even when you're not around.

Find a man who values you and who would never put themselves in a position to lose you.

Find a man who wakes up every day looking for new ways to love you.

Find a man that understands it's not about giving you the world but making you feel like you're the only one in it.

Remember your time is precious. Don't waste it on someone who doesn't realize you are too.

if you find such man, keep him no matter what

Pastor Kipkirui started this post off with these words, also, very good advice for all to listen to:

Young ladies arrived at a Meeting wearing clothes that were quite revealing their body parts.

Here is what the Chairman told them: He took a good look at them and made them sit down. Then he said something that they might never forget in their lives. He looked at them straight in the eyes and said; "ladies, everything that God made valuable in this world is well covered and hardly to see, to find or to get.

1. Where do you find Diamonds? Deep down in the ground, covered and protected.
2. Where do you find Pearls? Deep down at the bottom of the ocean, covered up and protected in a beautiful shell.
3. Where do you find Gold? Way down in the mine, covered over with layers of rock and to get them, you have to work hard & dig deep down to get them.

He looked at them with serious eyes and said;

"Your body is sacred & unique" You are far more precious than gold, diamonds and pearls, and you should be covered too." So he added that, if you keep your treasured mineral just like gold, diamond and pearls, deeply covered up, a reputable mining organization with the requisite machinery will fly down and conduct years of extensive exploration. First, they will contact your government (family), sign professional contracts (wedding) and mine you professionally (legal marriage). But if you leave your precious minerals uncovered on the surface of the earth, you always attract a lot of illegal miners to come and mine you illegally. Everybody will just pick up their crude instruments and just have a dig on you just freely like that. Keep your bodies deeply covered so that it will invite a professional miner to chase you up honorably.

Let's all encourage our wives, friends and daughters to dress well and decent!

Proverbs 31:10-31[1]

10 **Who can find a virtuous woman? For her price is far above rubies**.

> Virtuous: Righteous, good, moral, excellence, humility, charity, chaste. Any good quality, or admirable trait of character. To do willingly what must be done anyway.

11-12. **The heart of her husband doth safely trust in her, so that he shall have no need of spoil. She will do him good and not evil all the days of her life.**

- She never puts him down in front of others.
- Does the things that would be pleasing to him.
- Submits to his God given authority.
- He knows that if he asks her to do something, it will be done.
- She doesn't spend his hard-earned money foolishly.

---

[1] *All Scripture is from the King James Version, from the PC Study Bible 5 Cd except that under "other translations say". This info comes from The Bible from 26 Translations published by Baker. The other translations are: The Bible: An American Translation; Amplified; American Standard Version; Bible in Basic English; Modern Language Bible-New Berkeley Version; Jerusalem Bible, Holy Scriptures the Masoretic text; New American; New English; The Emphasized Bible; Revised Standard; The Living Bible; Young's Literal Translation of the Holy Bible. (Note, not all of these were necessarily quoted from.)*

13. **She seeketh wool, and flax, and worketh willingly with her hands**.

- SHE IS NOT LAZY!!!!!
- Keeps husband's, children's and own wardrobe in good repair. Makes sure everyone has what he or she needs. When adding to it, she considers wear-ability and the person's taste in clothing; something they like and you can live with, keeping it modest, yet tasteful. She also keeps the budget in mind.
- Keeps the house clean, a home to be proud of.

14-15. **She is like the merchants' ships; she bringeth her food from afar. She riseth also while it is yet night, and giveth meat to her household, and a portion to her maidens.**

She plans her family's meals with creativity, and the budget in mind. Follows the sales and gets the best buys. Stays informed of the latest nutritional findings and keeps her families health intact. She considers her family's likes and dislikes, when planning the menu. But, remembers, 'you can't please everyone all the time.'

16-19**. She considereth a field, and buyeth it: with the fruit of her hands she planteth a vineyard. She girdeth her loins with strength, and strengtheneth her arms. She perceiveth that her merchandise is good: her candle goeth not out by night. She layeth her hands to the spindle, and her hands hold the distaff.**

She considers her talents and abilities, putting them to good use. Working day and night, she builds a good business.

AFTER her family and home are taken care of, as we see by the preceding verses. She keeps in shape, so to stay strong and healthy.

20. **She stretcheth out her hand to the poor; yea, she reacheth forth her hands to the needy.**

Gives of her means to the poor. Helps the sick and disabled with their daily routines they can no longer do. Makes herself available to listen to problems and the needs of others. She is not afraid to go out of her way for someone. She does all joyfully and willingly.

21-25. **She is not afraid of the snow for her household: for all her household are clothed with scarlet. She maketh herself coverings of tapestry; her clothing is silk and purple. Her husband is known in the gates, when he sitteth among the elders of the land. She maketh fine linen, and selleth it; and delivereth girdles unto the merchant. Strength and honour are her clothing; and she shall rejoice in time to come.**

In the winter the family has warm clothing. Her dress becomes her, is modest and pleasing to her husband. She makes things to sell: sewing, cooking, crafts, etc. She is a woman of honor, one worthy of respect. She is happy, doesn't run around gloomy faced and ill tempered.

26-31. **She openeth her mouth with wisdom; and in her tongue is the law of kindness. She looketh well to the ways of her household, and eateth not the bread of idleness. Her children arise up, and call her blessed; her husband also, and he praiseth her. Many daughters have done virtuously, but thou excellest them all. Favour is deceitful, and beauty is vain: but a**

woman that feareth the Lord, she shall be praised. Give her of the fruit of her hands; and let her own works praise her in the gates.

She stays in the word of God, drawing strength from it daily. Gaining God's wisdom, she speaks and holds to the law of kindness. She keeps her children under control, and knows what they are doing with their spare time. She is never idle, but uses her time wisely. Her children and husband love and respect her. They praise her for all she does. Charm and beauty are on the surface, it's what's inside, that counts.

Some say this is not a woman, but the church. Personally, I don't see that connection. But, let's for arguments sake, say it is. I have one question, "Who is the church?" I'll even answer it. "We are; each one of us jointly and individually." As the church, we are each to be a virtuous wife (if you're a woman, the men are to be Godly husbands.) It isn't as hard as it seems. Take it a verse at a time and you will find that you are probably already doing most of the things she does.

PRESCRIPTION

Now that we have defined, what the virtuous wife is and does, how do we become her? In the chapters that follow, we will find out. I would suggest as you study each area, that you start applying it to your life.

This may mean taking a little longer (like two or three years) to finish the book, but your life will be greatly enriched by doing so. You don't have to completely conquer one area before moving on to the next, but be sure you're comfortable enough in it, so you don't lose it. Don't try to do too much too fast.

(If you're like me you're going to have to keep reading. Okay, if you must you must, you can always keep track of the pages you need to work on, but aren't ready to yet and come back to them later.)

Since each one will have some areas already conquered and varying degrees of needing work in others, you should move on at your own personal speed.

If doing the book in a study with others you may need to move on before you're ready. That's okay. Just keep working on what you need to work on and make a note of what the next step is for you. As a group, you will need to steadily work on the book, but as an individual, you need to steadily work on your life, and it will take a lot longer.

This is an ongoing process. *Don't stop, just because you finished the book.* Read it again, you're bound to have missed something the first time.

Before we get started, just let me remind you, this is not impossible! As Paul tells us in *Philippians 4:13*

I CAN DO ALL THINGS THROUGH CHRIST, WHO STRENGTHENS ME!

What's that you say? You've always done everything yourself. You don't need anyone's help. especially not a god who doesn't exist!

First, I would like to ask: "Why are you reading this book?" Second, "Has everything you have ever done come out the way you wanted it to?" "Are you happy with your life the way it is? Be honest, you're only fooling yourself."

You are right about one thing. You don't need the help of a god that doesn't exist, you need the help of THE ONE that does. Let's look to see what His Word says:

Romans 3:23

> **For all have sinned, and come short of the glory of God;**

Man IS sinful; every one of us has sinned and need to repent. Repent means to turn from and stop doing. Just saying, 'I'm sorry please forgive me' isn't enough. God looks at the heart. He knows if you mean it or not. You may be able to fool man, but you cannot fool God.

Romans 5:8-9

> **But God commendeth his love toward us, in that, while we were yet sinners, Christ died for us. Much more then, being now justified by his**

> **blood, we shall be saved from wrath through him.**

We cannot be justified by our own actions. It is only by/through Christ Jesus that we can be saved.

Romans 8:13

> **For if ye live after the flesh, ye shall die: but if ye through the Spirit do mortify the deeds of the body, ye shall live.**

Flesh = Sin/death Spirit = life

Romans 10:13

> **For whosoever shall call upon the name of the Lord shall be saved.**

1. Ask for forgiveness 2. Repent, turn away from your sin, don't look back, (don't go back to it.) 3. Accept God's free gift of Salvation.

Romans 10:17

> **So then faith cometh by hearing, and hearing by the word of God.**

READ YOUR BIBLE!!

John 3:16-18

> **For God so loved the world, that he gave his only begotten Son, that whosoever believeth in him should not perish, but have everlasting life. For God sent not his Son into the world to condemn**

> **the world; but that the world through him might be saved. He that believeth on him is not condemned: but he that believeth not is condemned already, because he hath not believed in the name of the only begotten Son of God.**

Believe in God = Knowing that He is God; He IS love, and He IS your Savior. Accept His love and free gift of Salvation.

Ephesians 2:8 & 9

> **For by grace are ye saved through faith; and that not of yourselves: it is the gift of God: Not of works, lest any man should boast.**

We are saved because of God's grace and love toward us; NOT because of anything we do or have done.

Revelation 3:19-21

> **As many as I love, I rebuke and chasten: be zealous therefore, and repent. Behold, I stand at the door, and knock: if any man hear my voice, and open the door, I will come in to him, and will sup with him, and he with me. To him that overcometh will I grant to sit with me in my throne, even as I also overcame, and am set down with my Father in his throne.**

Remember, this was written to those who believed, not to those still needing salvation. God wants to perfect us, and will take the time necessary to do so. He just asks you to let Him in and allow Him to do so.

"WHAT!" You might ask, "Does that have to do with the topic of this book?"

EVERYTHING!

Matthew 19:26b

> **With men this is impossible; but with God all things are possible.**

We cannot, by our own power, become virtuous wives. We can only do so through the power of God. In order for His power to work in us, He needs a clear channel, one free of sin.

If, while reading this you realize that you have not settled your account with God, now is the time to do so. All it takes is a very simple prayer, sincerity of heart, and belief that God is able to do all that He says.

Just repeat this prayer, or use one of your own. The words don't really matter. God looks at the heart.

> *Dear God,*
>
> *I realize that I am a sinner and deserve to spend eternity in hell. Thank-you for sending your Son to die for me, that I might live. Forgive me for the sins of my past and present, come live in me, and help me to do your will. Amen.*

Intro

Just a suggestion on how to use this book more productively. If possible, incorporate it into a group Bible study. At the start of the study, get a prayer partner. Keep in mind you don't want two "anything goes" or "it has to be perfect," types together. (Leaders, see Leader's Guide, at the back of this book, for more details.)

If you can't do the group study, at least get the prayer partner, she will be very important to your success! (See Leader's Guild for more details.)

Now that we have that settled, let's get started. Before getting into our scripture, we have a little prep work to do. So, let's start with getting a note book. Yep, that's right, you're going back to school, so take good notes and study hard so you can pass your test. □

We'll start with doing a self-evaluation. Fill in where you stand now, and your goal for where you want to be. The list below is a guide, it is not a comprehensive list, so add to it. You want as much in each area as you can think off to truly access where you are and where you want to be.

As you go through this book you will be adding new things. You may want to leave a few pages blank at the end of each area or just add new notes as they come up.

This is your notebook, do it the way that makes sense to you. You will also be using this book to answer the discussion questions at the beginning of each Chapter, and taking notes on each. So, maybe a loose-leaf notebook will be good so you can add pages as needed, where needed.

Self-Evaluation Form

SPIRITUAL:

Pray every day

One hour or more

Daily personal devotions

Daily family devotions

Daily walk

Personal Ministry

Church involvement

Treatment of family

Treatment of friends

Treatment of self

FAMILY:

Spend time together doing fun things as a family

Spend fun time with each person alone

Help each child attain his or her own spiritual walk with Christ

Health concerns – list each member of your family and their health problems.

Possible solutions to these health concerns.

Find each child's talent, gift, walk in life; and help him/her use it, grow in it.

Are you the "Help-meet" your husband needs? (Remember WE are to be HIS helper, not him Ours!)

Do your outside activities take too much time away from your family?

Family ministry

HOUSE:

- Are there things in your home that would not be pleasing to God?
    - Get rid of what you can, but if it is your husband's, it is his choice. Pray over these things.
- Junky closets?
    - Do you have a place for everything; Everything in its place?
- What are your problem areas?
    - Possible solutions

VIRTUES TO STRIVE FOR:

Make a list of the virtues you already have, and those you would like to have. As we go through the book you will probably be adding to this list, so you may want to leave room for additions.

Use the above as a guide, but don't limit yourself to only what is listed. You know what you need to do, figure out how to do it. If you're really at a loss right now, don't worry. As we work through this book, you'll get more ideas. (You may want to save room for them. Maybe skip a few pages here)

Example:

- Devotions – What do you need to study? What does your family need? By the topic? I/e Fruit of the Spirit, Family life, Prayer. By the Book? I/e Job, Titus, Psalms.

- Church involvement – Am I spending too much time or not enough? How can I help more at church without taking time from my family?

Time to get back to our text in Proverbs and once again take it section by section. This time in much greater detail, showing how to really apply it to our lives. If you follow the instructions, you will become the Virtuous Wife found in Proverbs 31.

Now, on to the book, I pray it blesses you.

Discussion 1

Who can find a virtuous woman? For her price is far above rubies. Pro. 31:10

1. Should we try to be the virtuous wife spoken of here or give up without trying? (We all know it's impossible for one woman to do all that! This woman is perfect, and it's humanly impossible to be that perfect. Right?)

2. What does being a virtuous wife entail?

3. How much are rubies worth?

4. Is our price (value) as an average wife today worth even that, let alone more?

5. Why is a *Virtuous* wife worth so much more?

6. Why is it important for a Christian woman to be the best wife, *by God's standards,* she can be?

7. When we change from our old contentious habits and become the loving virtuous wife, we all want to be, what kind of initial response can we expect from our husbands? Why?

8. What other spiritual laws will have a bearing on how he responds to you?

9. Does this mean we're fighting a losing battle?

10. Is a gradual or overnight total, all at once change better? Why?

(You can find my answers in Appendix I starting on page 139)

CH 1

Who can find a virtuous woman? For her price is far above rubies. Pro. 31:10

The best place to start anything is at the beginning. So, to become a virtuous wife, assuming you already are a wife, you must first become a virtuous woman.

As this verse implies, it is very hard to find one, so how do you become one? In this book we will find out and there will be many challenges along the way. I hope you are ready to face them and take them head on.

Let's get started. Here are a few suggestions for the first leg of this quest:

Do a word study on the words "Wife", "Virtuous", "Love" & "Marriage" and all words associated with them. Make a list of these qualities. Don't forget to look up the definition of each. As silly as this sounds, you find out some very interesting things by defining and doing word studies on very simple words. When you finish with Webster's, (The older dictionaries are better for this. The 1828 is excellent); go to your concordance. (If you don't have one, maybe you could borrow one from your church Library, Pastor, or a friend.)

1. (You can see my examples in Appendix 1 Page 139)

2. Honestly and prayerfully, with the help of your prayer partner, (you may want to get together for tea for this one) check off the qualities from the above study that you have already mastered. Then list those remaining in the order that you need to, (not want to), work on them.

3. Do a word study on virtuous wives and their characteristics. This will take a long time to go through all the women of the Bible. Maybe you could do two women a week and if going through this study with a group, discuss what you find while doing that week's chapter study. You may find that studying the un-virtuous wives may also be a big help. Sometimes, we find out what not to do by seeing what happens when someone does it. Add to your list in number 1 & 2 as you find new qualities to consider.

Virtuous Women Study – example:

Key :

Numbered entries = Virtuous traits

- = Un-virtuous traits

  - ○ = Ways to correct bad traits

Eve: Genesis

- Listened to the lie and was easily deceived. 3:1-6
  - Study the word so you cannot be so easily deceived. Be careful not to mis-quote it, as Eve did in v.3 (see Gen. 2:17)

Eve may not have misquoted the Word. She, or Adam may have put a fence around it. This is something the Priests used to do; to help people from falling into sin. If the command was 'do not lust' they would say 'do not look'. This would have been done with good intentions and it is believed that Jesus did this as well (They say...but I say) But, in this case it could have been Eve's downfall. 'Don't even touch or you will die.' But the snake touched it and he didn't die, 'so maybe I can eat it too?'

1. Repented, (Understood from 4:1, because she recognized the blessing of a son as a gift from God.)
2. ...

Noah's Wife and Daughters-in Law: Genesis 6:12-7:19

1. Stood by her (Their) husband(s) (and father-in-law) when everyone else mocked them

2. Worked with him to fulfill what God said to do.

3. Believed in him

4. Did not complain ...

By doing two women a week you will not get through all the woman of the Bible by the time you finish this book. So, you may want to continue doing your two women a week when you finish this book and move on to something else.

4. Now, ask yourself, "Am I closer to being a wife of the Word or a wife of the world? (Keep in mind here, my answer to Discussion Question 4. The object is to start assessing yourself honestly, to see yourself as God sees you, so you can become whom He wants you to be.

5. Take your list and start on them one at a time, as we go through this book together. This may take a while, but it can be done, while you work on other things. Add things to do with the house or some other area. Never work on too many things in the same area at the same time. This is a long process, but if you work steadily at it, you will find yourself becoming a wife of the Word.

Apply the qualities you found in your study of the word "Virtuous" to your role as wife and mother. If you have children, I believe these roles go hand in hand. Your actions as a mother will be reflected in your actions as a wife and visa/versa. As you will remember, the children are mentioned in this Scripture also; more on that later.

This may be the hardest part of all you have to do. The devil knows you mean business and he does not want you to succeed. He knows the more ground you gain the harder it will be to deter you, or to sway you from your goal. He will pull out all the stops now, trying to make you fail before you begin. DON'T let him!

Don't hide what's happening from your prayer partner. If you feel like giving up, tell her so; then, PRAY THROUGH IT TOGETHER! God WILL give you the victory! DO NOT GIVE UP! If you still can't break through call your Church's prayer chain.

If you don't have a church Prayer chain, start one. Meanwhile, call everyone you can. You don't have to give details, just say, "Pray for me, keep praying for me." Tell them you are fighting a spiritual battle. Don't abuse this chain; it should be for emergencies only. Spiritual warfare is an emergency, but be sure it is Spiritual warfare and not laziness.

Especially, but not only, if you have an unsaved spouse, satan will use him. While you're working on one area to relive stress and tension in the home, he will be complaining about another, perhaps one he has never complained about before. Recognize it as a spiritual battle, take a deep breath and go to your battlefield, the prayer closet.

Remember, satan wants you to scream back. Don't give him the satisfaction. If you must, bite your tongue; and when you have a sufficient hole therein, PRAY.

Do not let him make your marriage the battlefield. Remember, your husband is the head of your home, saved or not, respect him as such. Satan would like nothing more than to make you come out from under his authority, disrespect him, not submit to him, start and or continue arguments.

This is one of the quickest ways to destroy a marriage and witness, not to mention causing you to blaspheme.

Titus 2:5 To be discreet, chaste, keepers at home, good, <u>obedient to their *OWN* husbands, that the word of God be not blasphemed</u>. KJV)

Satan would like nothing better. Don't give him the foothold.

One more thing to remember, satan likes to come in that forgotten door. So, while you're working on one area you may be surprised at how easy it was to conquer. Then months later, when you've tackled five others and you're working on number six, in he comes to bring that one from months earlier back. He may be there slowly working away at it for weeks before you realize, but don't despair. The Bible tells us:

"SUBMIT YOURSELVES THEREFORE TO GOD, RESIST THE DEVIL, AND HE WILL FLEE FROM YOU. James 4:7

Submit to God: Do what He says, read His word, line your life up with Him, Put Him first in your life, Keep divine order, etc.

Resist the devil: don't listen to him, don't engage conversation with him, tell him to leave, start praying, listen to Good Christian music, sing praises to God.

He WILL flee: go away, run!

This is a test. This is only a test. For the next 30 seconds (days, months, years,) this marriage will be conducting a test. We will be back in full swing as soon as I prove I can trust God to see me through, and not give into these lies.

There are many scriptures dealing with submission and several talk of submission one to another, and submission to God. Most people don't have a problem with these; they will agree that it should be so. BUT, talk about a wife submitting to her husband! Look out! World War three is on the brink! All the excuses come out:

- You can't submit to someone that's not saved, that's like submitting to the devil.
    - God says: **1 Peter 3:1-2 Likewise, ye wives, be in subjection to your own husbands; that, if any obey not the word, they also may without the word be won by the conversation of their wives; While they behold your chaste conversation coupled with fear. KJV**
        - Conversation here is not your words but rather your behavior, how you conduct yourself.
- You're supposed to submit to God and if my husband says something that's wrong than I can't do it, I have to follow God.
    - God tells us to submit to our husband, so are you following God if you don't? (We'll talk more about these two later.)

- But I have a right to my opinion! If he's in the wrong, I should be able to point that out. And if he does it at the top of his voice, I can do it at the top of mine. After all, I should be heard too. I do have rights!
    - God had rights; He gave them up for us; can't you give yours up for Him? The quicker we give up our rights the quicker we will find true happiness.
- But I have to protect my rights. If I don't no one else will.
    - HOGWASH! God will protect your rights. You need to be submissive to Him and do what He says. (Throughout this book we will discover what God says, and commands us to do.)
- But when he's drunk, he's a different man and he makes demands that I can't live with. How can I submit to that?
    - This requires a slightly different approach. You need to understand true submission. As you said, he is a different man, not the one you married, the one you promised to love, honor, and obey. Not the one God called you to submit to. You need to stay submissive, but you submit to what he would want if he were sober. If you are truly submissive to him in all things when he is sober, God will get him to back down when he is drunk. But, when you tell him you don't want to do what he is asking, do it in love, in a spirit of submission. Don't return anger for anger. Be quiet, loving, submissive. And PRAY that God

will intervene, let Him deal with your husband and get him to change his mind. That is NOT your job.

Before we go on, let's talk a little about what submission is and isn't:

- Submission is NOT about one having power over another.

- Submission does NOT equal "doormat"

- Submission does NOT happen when someone insists you do something.

➢ Submission is a choice one makes and freely gives to another.

  - I can choose to submit; you can NOT force me to submit.

  - If it is forced, it becomes abuse.

  - God does not want us to be abused, or to live with abuse.

All things work together for good to those who love the Lord and are called according to His purpose. (Romans 8:28)

We are called to be virtuous wives, therefore in our struggle to attain that calling, we can be assured that everything will work together for good. Even what satan tries to destroy, will come out perfected. Maybe not the way we think it should, but if we are truly seeking the Lord's will in our life, He will lead us where He wants us. So, let's get started!

We've been talking about being virtuous, and are all looking forward to that high calling. But sometimes it's good to know what we need to come out of, to get a better view of what we are coming in to. So, what is the opposite of virtuous? Could it be contentious?

Are you contentious? If you:

- Criticize often
- Rant and rave
- Continually remind him of things
- Go on and on about nothing
- Talk a mile a minute about nothing
- Give him a list of things to do every day
- Etc. etc. etc.

Then, you are a contentious wife. So, what can be done about it?

1. Stop criticizing. Start edifying. Build your husband up.
    a. Tell him how much you love him. Show him with little things: His favorite meal; special dessert; back rub; cup of coffee or tea; etc.
2. Talk often about the good things he does. Remember to say thank-you for even the smallest things he does for you. Let him know that he is appreciated.
    a. Stop talking about the negative things he does, or the things you don't like. Tell your friends about the good stuff not the bad stuff. It will get back to him and it will have an effect.

3. Sit down with him and say nothing; let him start the conversation. Ask him how his day went and let him do the talking. He will probably be so used to you doing all the talking that he won't know what to say or do. Don't fill up the silence with chatter, wait for him to talk then really listen. Let him know you care about what he has to say.

4. If something needs to be done, try to do it yourself. Only pass on the things you can't do; ONE at a time. Ask him nicely, ONE time. Don't bring it up again unless he's had two or three days off and hasn't done it. Then just ask if he's had time to look at it yet, maybe offer to help him when he's ready and drop the subject.

This may sound like nothing will ever get done. Stay calm, relax, PRAY, let God deal with your husband and you. The number one objective is to stop nagging. If things in the house don't get done for a while, that's a small price to pay.

Your husband expects you to start nagging and is waiting for you to do so. That's his excuse not to do anything. So don't hand him his excuses, instead, give him a loving patient wife. Soon he will be mad at himself for not doing that one little thing you asked of him.

If you must make out that "Honey Do..." list, do so. When you have the 150 items written down, tuck it away in your drawer and cross them off as they get done. But, DON'T - EVER – GIVE - HIM the list. Men cringe when they see a list of things to do written out.

So, we are all in agreement, we want to stop being contentious and start being virtuous. Remember one of the definitions of virtuous is to do willingly what must be done anyways. Have you ever worked with someone that was constantly complaining about their job?

It makes me want to scream, 'just go away, I'll do it myself.' I hate being around someone who is constantly complaining as I'm sure you do. So, if you are sweeping the floor for the fiftieth time today, remember, it needs to be done; so, just do it.

No one wants to hear you complaining; not even you. The job will get done faster and better if you do it with a good attitude. You'll be a lot happier too.

You are now on your way to becoming good, chaste, righteous, virtuous. The very things that just last week sent you crawling up the walls. You are becoming the person you used to hate. And why did you hate her so much? Because you knew, you should be like her but didn't know how to attain that lofty position. Now that you know it's not impossible, it feels pretty good. Doesn't it?

Other translations say:

1. Instead of "Virtuous:

- "Worthy" (ASV & NAB)
    - Although worthy (-ily) is listed in the Strongs as an acceptable translation for the original Hebrew word, I keep thinking "None are worthy, no not one." There is a big difference between being worthy and being virtuous. When you are worthy than you are "deserving". In the case of being worthy to be someone's wife, sometimes

that will be a very easy thing, in some cases he isn't worthy of you, but that doesn't mean that you are virtuous.

- "Wife with Strength of Character (Ber)
    - This is a little better, your strength of character remains the same no matter what the circumstance. But still, it is only part of what Virtuous is.
- The Hebrew word is: *Chayil* – (Strongs Concordance)
    - a force, whether of men, means or other resources; an army, wealth, virtue, valor, strength: able activity, (+) army, band of men (shoulders), company, (great) forces, host, might, power, riches, strength, strong, substance, train (+) valiant (-ly), valor, virtuous (-ly), war, worthy (-ily).

2. Instead of "Price":

- Worth (RHM)
    - This is still an accurate translation here.
- "Far more precious than" (BER)
    - It doesn't have quite the same feel somehow. You can be precious to someone but not be very good for them.

3. Instead of "Rubies":

- "Pearls" (SPRL & NAB); "Corals" (RHM); "Jewels" (BAS & BER); or "Has an unfailing prize"
    - Some of these sounds innocent enough. The Hebrew word is *"Paniy"* – probably a pearl (as round); - Ruby.
    - So, what difference does it make if you say "pearl", "Ruby" or "jewel? Not much. It's just that the Ruby is the *most costly and precious* of all jewels. So, do you want to be just one of many jewels? Or do you want to become the most precious?

Discussion 2

The heart of her husband doth safely trust in her, so that he shall have no need of spoil. She will do him good and not evil all the days of her life.

Pro. 31:11-12

1. There are some people who won't trust anyone, no matter what. Can you force a man like that to trust you?

2. What are some things you can do to show that you can be trusted?

3. How do our husbands "Spoil"?

4. What good can you do your husband?

CH 2

The heart of her husband doth safely trust in her, so that he shall have no need of spoil. She will do him good and not evil all the days of her life. Pro. 31:11-12

Trust is more important in marriage, than any other relationship. If you don't trust a friend, you watch what you say in front of them. If you don't trust your boss, you can find another job. If you don't trust your employee, you can fire him. But, when you don't trust your spouse, you lose that solid ground you need to build a good marriage. Despite what the world says, you can't just go out and find another one!

How can you regain the trust you lost a long time ago? You have to convince your husband that you can be trusted ONE STEP AT A TIME. He probably won't even consider trusting you for at least a month after you start showing that you can be trusted. Total trust will take a lot longer. Don't give up, prove yourself and the trust will come. Remember, you have years to make up for and everybody knows old habits die hard.

When your husband asks you to do something, no matter how trivial, make that your number one priority. Remember, you can't be trusted in the big things until you've proven yourself in the small. Don't stop trying, and don't continually nag him with, "You can trust me now, you know." Let him see it in your actions, not your words.

Don't talk about him behind his back. Don't talk negatively about your friends, or his friends, or family. (If you talk about them, he will feel that you will talk about him too, and probably you will.)

Remember the old adage, "If you can't say something nice don't say anything at all." That is a good rule to live by. In the past you use to put him down every chance you got; never saying anything good about him, in public or private. Now you have to watch your words every second. Sharpen those teeth; they have a very thick, bitter tongue to bite through.

You have degraded your husband worse than any human deserves to be. It will be a long time before he will trust you with his emotions again. All hope is not lost. We serve a God who is still in the miracle working business! He does the impossible.

Your husband can be won back. Start by telling him you love him. Show him your love by doing special things for him throughout the week. (I know it's the man that is usually told to do this for his wife, but it works both ways.) If the feelings aren't there now, pray and ask God to manifest them within you. He will. Believe me! HE WILL!!

Side note: My first marriage was not the best by any means, and at one point I had had all I could take and just wanted out. I told the Lord; "I don't love my husband and I don't want to." He said, "Let Me love him through you." I said okay, and the next two weeks were the best weeks of our entire marriage.

I didn't actually do anything different, or at least I didn't think I did, but my husband responded to God loving him through me. But, at last, he was not saved and it wasn't enough to change him, life went back to the way it was, and I found myself more alone than ever, with 2 children and another on the way. (But then I didn't do much changing either. It was before I started this book and I had much to learn.)

Two or three years later I again wanted out. God again said "let Me love him through you." But this time I said no. I don't want another two weeks of a good marriage just to have everything go back to this. It was then that God taught me unconditional love.

Our marriage never got any better, but my attitude changed. I didn't like him much, but I could honestly say I loved him. Not the kind of love you need to make a good marriage, you need two people working together to make a good marriage, and he wasn't interested. But that is another very long story. Perhaps I'll tell it someday, but this book is not the place.

The lesson here is, don't give up until you have tried everything possible. Yes, there are some marriages that can't be saved, because one or both parties are not willing to invest the time or effort it will take. But don't be the one that gives up. As long as both are willing to work at it any marriage can be saved. And some have been saved in spite of the opposition. (End of Rabbit trail #1)

Perhaps you could make a special dinner one night and take a stroll down Memory Lane. Talk about things you used to do together that you both enjoyed. Talk of things he used to do that you really appreciated; of things you used to do, "and why did we stop?" Chances are he misses those times too. Perhaps you could ignite the old spark again.

Your next step is to stop criticizing your husband and start edifying him, lifting him up every chance you get; in private and public. For years you've let him know what you don't like about him, now let him know what you do like.

If your marriage has gotten really bad and there's not a lot left that you do like, start digging, there has to be something. Hey, guess what! He's working; bringing home money; putting food on the table, say thank-you. Or, maybe you're able to slip through the door before him, when he opens it. Say "Thank you."

Add this to your list of things to work on. Find at least one new thing about your husband, (and each child) to be thankful for each week. Perhaps this could be your dinner conversation. Let everyone hear what wonderful things each one has done that day.

The more personal you get here the better. But if you're not ready for that, start small and work up. Don't settle for skimming the surface here. You have to keep digging, keep talking until you are both comfortable with giving and receiving compliments. Take it one step at a time. Remember, we're breaking old habits here, ones that don't want to be broken. You've been exercising that tongue a long time and it doesn't want to stop exercising.

This may be a good time to do a study on James. If you've been letting your tongue run wild against your husband, you've probably let it go in other areas too. Curbing it now in those areas could help you with your husband also. Please, if you've been avoiding James 3, take it out now and ask God to reveal all He wants you to know and do concerning the tongue. I'm sure someone must have written an excellent book on this subject. Find it, read it. Let God work through and in you. Of course, you can start with the mini study below. Remember:

James 1:26

> **If any man among you seem to be religious, and bridleth not his tongue but deceiveth his own heart, this man's religion is vain.**

Now, on to the study:

James 3 – The Tongue

(When there is a Scripture reference written in bold print, read that portion of Scripture before continuing.)

James 3:1-2 We are first warned that most of us should not be teachers. (Masters here means teachers) Why?

Because teachers will receive a greater condemnation, or judgment.

This does not mean that when we teach other's things from the Word of God correctly, that we will be condemned for doing so. The condemnation comes in when we teach false doctrine, or when we teach the truth, but don't practice it ourselves.

The first, because we are leading others astray, the second, because we know the truth of what we say, but deny it in our own life.

James goes on to say that this condemnation comes, because we offend all in many things. Most offenses will usually come in one of the two ways listed above. Another big offense comes, when we preach the truth, but lack the love.

When you correct someone, they aren't very likely to take what you have to say very well, if they sense you don't really care about them. Even if they know what you are saying is 100% true, they will be more apt to throw it out the window.

BUT, if you speak the truth in love; be firm, yet gentle, loving, kind; then they will be more apt to receive it, no matter how hard it is for them to accept. Many will thank you for caring enough to say something.

Why is this warning the first thing said in a discussion on the tongue? Because, teachers can be great offenders with their tongue. Everyone needs to watch what they say and how they say it, but teachers have a greater audience, therefore, the damage that could be done is greatly multiplied.

So, here is the opening that gets us to the point of this chapter. "Many WILL offend in word." Those who don't are perfect and able to control their whole body, every aspect of their life.

This is why controlling the tongue is so important to a virtuous wife. We need to be in control of ourselves for we have a great responsibility placed on us.

James 3:3-4 These two comparisons are very interesting. They talk of how something very small can control something 50 to 1000 times its size. It doesn't seem possible, yet we all know the truth of these examples.

So, what point is James making? It's so obvious, I really don't have to say it, but I will. Our tongue; though small in size, can and does control our whole body, our whole life. Our tongue determines how others see us and what they will think of us. We MUST learn to control it.

But God does not want us to be bridled. **Ps. 32:8-9** He will guide us and teach us, if we will but listen to Him. And He wants to do so with just a look. He wants us so in tune to Him, that we don't even need words. Don't be stubborn, needing the bit to pull you in the right direction. Pay attention and listen to God.

James 3:5-8 We might as well stop right here then. James just told us "The tongue is unruly and cannot be tamed, so why waste our time? Right?

The key here is that no MAN can tame it. But we know God is able. If we give our life and our tongue to Him, He will show us how to tame it, and how to live righteously before Him.

If you are unable to speak, don't think you're immune to this disease. You have a form of communication, and that form, for all intents and purposes, is your tongue. So, you can't get away from this study that easily.

I like James' choice of words here, "The tongue is a little member and boasteth great things." When do we get into the most trouble? When we start boasting. When you boast about how great you are, you show how small you are. The truly great ones seemingly don't know it.

Have you ever started a campfire? You start with some kindling wood, or if you're really good at it, like me, you might start with some crumbled up paper or dry leaves. Then you work up to the little twigs and eventually get to the kindling, then to the big logs. The thing to do is keep feeding it little by little, until it catches on really good. Soon, it can get out of control if you don't keep an eye on it.

The same thing can happen with your tongue. If you keep feeding it with a little gossip here, an off-color joke there, and a little white lie occasionally, before you know it, it will be out of control. It will be running all over town and you will find yourself saying things that just a few short weeks ago you would have never thought of saying.

James 3:9-12 It is impossible for two opposites to occupy the same space at the same time. For one will cancel out the other. If it is dark and you turn on a light, the light will take over the darkness and it will no longer be dark. If you have a glass of salt water and a glass of fresh water, and combine them, the salt will take over the fresh so that it will no longer be fresh.

If you have love for a friend and become angry at her, allowing bitterness to come in, it will displace the love. If you start praising and worshiping God, then turn your thoughts to something that causes you to become angry, you are no longer praising God.

I can see James as he delivers this message to the people he has grown to love. With tears streaming down his face, he turns to them saying, "My dear brothers, with your mouth you praise God, and with that same mouth, you tear down your neighbors. This should not be. My dear friends, how can you say you love God, when you can't even get along with your brothers?

John told us in I John 4:20, "if a man say, I love God, and hateth his brother, he is a liar; for he that loveth not his brother whom he hath seen, how can he love God, whom he have not seen?" God is love, and he teaches us to love. If we do not have the love of the Father in us for those around us, then we do not know the Father.

James 3:13-18 Many people have a problem with anger, envy, bitterness. They try to justify it by calling it "Righteous Anger." But, is it truly righteous anger? Ephesians 4:26-27 tells us, "Be angry and sin not; let not the sun go down upon your wrath; neither give place to the devil."

Is your "righteous anger" causing you to be bitter, or resentful? Do you find yourself wishing harm on another instead of praying for their salvation? If so, it is not "Righteous Anger".

A righteous anger will move you to hate the sin, but love the sinner. It will move you to have compassion on those that wish to, or have done, you harm. It will pull you to your knees, in tears, for the soul that is so far gone, that he doesn't know where to turn. A righteous anger draws you to God, not away from Him.

Also see: **I Peter 3:10; Psalms 12:2-5; & Proverbs 12:12-22** (end sermonette)

So, you always come and go as you please, never asking for, nor accepting your husband's opinion of what you should do. After all, women today are independent, and can do anything a man can do. We have finally obtained our long desired and deserved, freedom!! Why would you want to lose it all by asking for HIS permission?!!

BECAUSE GOD TELLS US TO!

Remember, your husband should never have to question where you are going or why. He shouldn't have to wonder if you are going where you say you are, or how long you'll be. He shouldn't have to question rather what you are doing is actually a good thing. AND he shouldn't have to worry about you every time you leave the house, because he doesn't know where you are. That is common courtesy; you would expect the same from him.

Ephesians 5:22-24 & 33b

> **Wives, submit yourselves unto your own husbands, as unto the Lord. For the husband is**

> **the head of the wife, even as Christ is the head of the church: and he is the savior of the body. Therefore as the church is subject unto Christ, so let the wives be to their own husbands in every thing. ...and the wife see that she reverence her husband.**

Some translations say "adapt yourselves to your husbands." It's a lot easier to "adapt" yourself, than it is to "Submit" yourself. But that isn't what God is telling us to do. God wants a people who are committed. A partial obedience is not commitment. (It also isn't real obedience.) God wants us to "Submit" to our husband's God given authority. He has placed him as head of the family and it is up to us to follow God's rules, not make up our own.

1 Peter 3:1-2

> **Likewise, ye wives, be in subjection to your own husbands; that, if any obey not the word, they also may without the word be won by the conversation of the wives; While they behold your chaste conversation coupled with fear.**

Another translation actually says it pretty well; "May be won by the daily life of their wives" (Wey)

Conversation here means general course of conduct, or behavior. Lest you think this was only Paul, or his influence, let's go back to the garden:

Genesis 3:16

> **Unto the woman he said, I will greatly multiply thy sorrow and thy conception; in sorrow thou**

shalt bring forth children; and thy desire shall be to thy husband, and he shall rule over thee.

Yes, this was part of a curse. But, tell me, what is so bad about having someone taking care of you, looking out for you, protecting you, loving you? God, in His wisdom, gave us exactly what we needed. The women who are truly happy are those who have accepted their position in the Lord and see it for what it truly is; a blessing.

Besides, when you really study that scripture through, you realize that God was turning things back to the way they were intended to be in the first place. Remember, Eve was made from Adam's side. He was to be her protector; and she was to be his helper.

Yes; and how about that new dress you want. Of course, you deserve it and we both know the twenty you have hanging in the closet won't make it through the month. Besides, if it was something he wanted, even at twice the cost, he wouldn't hesitate to buy it.

SOUR GRAPES! Don't bother trying to eat them, just throw them away. If he says no, that is your answer, even if you only have one very old dress in your closet. It may not seem fair, but then it doesn't have to be. (Keep in mind; we're not talking about controlling, abusive husbands here. That is a different matter and has nothing to do with submission.)

Money is a very touchy subject in most marriages. I think most would agree that God's way is the best way, at least as long as you don't mention the tithe, or it doesn't go against what you want.

I believe, as head of the house, man is also in charge of the finances. That doesn't mean that woman can't pay the bills and do the bookkeeping, as long as she does it the way he wants. He should always know the condition of the finances, good or bad, and be consulted on major purchases and planning the budget.

In families I've known, where the wife ran everything and the husband didn't know where they stood financially, there were a lot of other problems in the home that got straightened out when this area was made right. Even when things were doing good, things got better when the husband took control. Remember, he is the head of the home. It is not your place to make any final decisions. You should have a say in the planning process, but it is his responsibility to decide how, what and when things will be done.

Since writing this book I have gotten some really good teaching on women and the whole aspect of submission and marriage. I want to share that here, so I decided to do a mini study on it:

Can Women Lead?

I have been taking some courses through The online teaching institution, *The Israel Bible Center.* They have a lot of excellent teachings; I would highly recommend to anyone. You can get their info in Appendex II of this book.

This study came as a result of one of those courses; "Women and Gender in The Bible" with Dr. Nicholas J. Schaser. It will give you another prospective, and maybe totally confuse all of us. ☺ You will have to take his course to get a better grasp of this. The original words and meanings I use here I gleaned from His course.

First let's get a better understanding of how the first woman was made and some of the words that will shed a brighter light on a woman's roll.

Gen 2:18 And the Lord God said, It is not good that the man should be alone; I will make him an help meet for him. KJV

The original language here is "ezer k'negdo". The Hebrew word "ezer" translates as helper. Most of the time, the Bible uses this word to describe God as a helper of humanity. The term describes God as being powerful, assertive, and strong.

The Hebrew k'negdo refers to standing before another in an equal relationship. So, putting them together you find that woman is an equal partner with the man, a mirror image, and strong helper.

Gen 2:21 And the Lord God caused a deep sleep to fall upon Adam and he slept: and he took one of his ribs, and closed up the flesh instead thereof; KJV

The original Hebrew word translated rib here is "tsela". However, this word never means "rib" in the Bible; rather, it means a complete "side." The woman was made from the man's complete side, not just one rib, which is why Adam was able to say "she is bone of my bone AND flesh of my flesh."

The word for sleep in this verse is "tardemah" which refers to the kind of "sleep" in which one sees visions and receives information from God (cf. Gen 15:1, 12; Job 4:13; 33:15; Isa 29:10-11). In the ancient Greek translation of the Hebrew Scriptures, the word the translator uses for "tardemah" is "ekstasis," which means "to stand outside." In the Greek version, Adam is literally "standing outside" himself and watching God create the woman in a visionary experience!

While Adam was in this deep sleep God took his side to make Eve and then rebuilt Adam's side. "Closed up" in the above verse is from the Hebrew "sagar" the same word used in I Kings 11:27 where Solomon closed up, or rebuilt the gap in the city wall.

One Flesh, in Gen. 2:24 and flesh of my flesh in Gen. 2:23a means person of my person; equal partner.

Now we can move on to some of the women leaders in Scripture. There are several women talked about in the Old Testament and a few in the New Testament that had very influential positions.

Miriam, the sister of Moses led the women in song and dance throughout their pilgrimage to the Promised land. Although Moses and Aaron were the main leaders at this time, Miriam was with them and was given some prophetic messages for the people. Some say she was the leader of the women. I can't find that spelled out in scripture, but it would stand to reason.

Deborah was a prophetess and a Judge. Some say the best judge in Israel's history. She used to set under the palm of Deborah between Ramah and Bethel in the hill country of Ephraim, where the people would come to her for judgments.

I have always assumed that this palm tree was on her and her husband's property. I don't know if that is true or not, or if anybody today really knows.

Deborah is known as the wife of Lappidot. In most English translations 'Lappidot' means flames, so another translation could be "woman of flames".

Judges were the rulers of Israel at this time, so that made Deborah the ruler. As you know, I have a little problem with this. I still find it hard to believe a woman was in a high position of leadership over men. But I'm not saying it wasn't possible or wasn't true.

Think about what happened when Barak refused to go to war, unless Deborah went too. He was the general of the Israel army and should have gotten credit for the victory; but because he insisted on Deborah going with him, that glory went to a woman. Seems like a slap in the face to me.

But yet at that time, the rulers usually led the army to battle. So, if Deborah truly was the ruler, perhaps it was her place to go and lead the battle. If so, wouldn't she have just done so instead of having to be talked into going by Barak? And wouldn't she have been honored with the kill?

Anna, was a prophetess who was at the temple when Marry and Joseph came in with baby Jesus. She told all who would listen about Jesus.

Then there was Priscilla and Aquila who taught Apollos, and held a home church. Many believe that Priscilla led the services, because she is mentioned first. To me that is a dangerous assumption, since it doesn't really tell us who led the services, just that they both ministered to people. Although, people with a lot more knowledge of that time period than I have, have made that suggestion, so maybe they are right???

I had always assumed that Aquila took the lead and Priscilla helped in his ministry. Then, there's the fact that this took place in their home, one on one so to speak. Not in a group setting.

This is really the only thing we know about their ministry from the bible. You may be able to find more on them in other books. I haven't done that research.

There were many women who followed Jesus along with the men. Many of them were wealthy and funded His ministry. They continued to fund the disciples after His death.

Many of the disciples took their wives with them when they went on ministry trips, although we don't hear of their participation, we know from Paul that they did go.

It is commonly believed that it was inappropriate for Jewish men to interact with woman not of their household. This is not true. Although, many believe otherwise, many Jewish men respected the thoughts and ideas of women.

Those who believe this will say that is the reason women were not to teach men. Those who know this is not true will say, so it is okay for women to teach men.

Dorcas, was a woman of many great works. She made many garments and other things for many people. But she ministered mostly to the women, especially the widows.

Many will say that because God said he would pour out His Spirit on all flesh, and sons and daughters would prophesy, that that proves it is acceptable for women to preach and teach men. But, prophesying is not the same as teaching or preaching.

Romans 16 lists many people who were workers in the Church, among them many women. But, there again, they were workers, nothing says that any of them taught or preached. Yes, they were great workers, leaders, but there are many different ministries that do not involve teaching and/or preaching.

Many think that Paul was always putting women down, not allowing them to have a position in ministry. This is not so. He praised many women for the work they did in the church, calling them co-workers, making them his equals.

In Ephesians 5:20-25 Paul tells the wives to submit to their own husbands, as to the Lord. Many get upset with this, but they miss that, husbands are told to love their wives as Christ loved the church and gave Himself for it. That is the deepest kind of submission.

I often wondered why he told wives to submit and husbands to love. Then it hit me, submission is a form of respect, if a man is not respected, he does not feel loved; a woman needs to know she is loved or she will not feel respected.

I Corinthians 14 is the scripture that gets Paul into the most trouble with woman. I believe mostly because of misunderstandings. In verse 34a he says: "Let your women keep silence in the churches; for it is not permitted for them to speak; ..."

There are many theories on this. Some say it is only the married women, because later he says let them ask their husbands at home if they don't understand something.

But why would the unmarried women be allowed to ask questions if the married one's aren't? Shouldn't they ask their fathers at home?

Then, some say it is only for the women prophets. But other scriptures tell us that women and men will prophecy in the church.

The theory that makes the most sense to me is one I had never heard before doing the study I mentioned at the start of this lesson. It is possible that this is a belief of the Corinthian church and Paul is quoting that here, since later he says: v.36 "What? Came the word of God out of you? Or came it onto you only?..."

In several ancient manuscripts v. 34-35 was put in after v. 40. If you take them out it does read smoother, and seems to better line up with other scriptures. Read I. Cor.14: 29-33, 36-40 then 34-35 and see for yourself.

One thing I have yet to see anyone look at is the word "Speak" When I looked this up in the Strong's Concordance one of the meanings was "Preach". Could it be that he meant women were not to preach in a church setting? That would fit with them not having authority over men.

I Tim. 2:14 is another problematic verse. It blames Eve for being deceived and not Adam, yet elsewhere Paul blames Adam. (Romans 5:12; & I Cor. 15:22)

While I greatly respect the teachers at the Israel Bible Center and have learned a lot from them, I am not in total agreement with them on this issue.

I agree women can be and are used mightily by God in many ministries, in and out of the church. They are equal partners with men and their own husbands, but I do not believe they should be in a position over men in the church.

Yes, they may know more than some men and can help men better understand the Scriptures. One on one, if the man asks for her help, I see nothing wrong with that. But in a group setting I think she needs to follow the chain of command: God, man, women, children.

In a Bible study environment, there is nothing wrong with her voicing her opinion, or expounding on the Scriptures, but there should be a man leading it, (Unless it is a women's or children's Bible Study.)

Yes, we all are to submit to one another and there is no difference between men and women IN Christ. But IN the home and IN the Church, I feel that man should be IN charge.

They should of course, respect the women in the assembly and hear what they have to say. Many times, they have better insights then the men. But still, I believe God placed man as head of the Home and Church. (Christ is head of the Church, but I think man is head of the workings of the church.)

When you think about it, Christ should be the head of the home as well, yet no one ever corrects you when you say man is head of the home. Many do, when you say man is head of the church. In both places, man should be listening to God and following His lead, (and so should woman).

Remember the symbolism: man represents God, Woman represents the church. The Church is NEVER above God. So, in the chain of command, women should NOT be above men. (End sermonette)

This study slightly changed my view on some of this, but not all. I hope it helps to clarify things a little more for you, and not just leave you more confused.

This next line really intrigues me. "He shall have no need of spoil." When you think of something as being spoiled you think of rotten food, or a child who got everything he ever thought he wanted, or whose parents gave in to him on everything.

Neither would have much to do with you and your husband. If he is spoiled, it was his parents, not you that did it. Or, was it?

There's an old saying, "All men are babies." When the truth is told, they are only babies in the eyes of their mothers and or wives, and quite often because these women refuse to let them be men. This ought not to be so.

Yes, there are a few men that refused to grow up long before they got married, but wives; you can make a difference. Let them know you need them to be grown men. Nicely, gently, lovingly let them know they can no longer be children.

When they got married, they became the head of their family, and they must take that position now. As long as you're taking the lead, correcting his mistakes, and doing things your way, you're not giving God a chance to correct him. So, it's time to back off and let God deal with him.

The Strong's Concordance lists another possible word for the one translated here as "Spoil." That word is "Prey." Have you made your husband your prey? Making him the victim?

Some husbands are very nice and want to give their wives everything they ask for and will do so at all costs. Many wives take advantage of that great generous spirit. Of course, I'm sure no one reading this book is like that; but, if you are, remember; just because your husband will give you anything you want, that doesn't mean you should ask for it, or take all he offers.

We have been assuming this was about money, or personality and the like. Another interpretation could be success in the business world. Do we really have any influence there? After all, it's his job. What happens to him there depends on him, right?

Yes, your husband's character and work habits will either take him far at work, or keep him job-hopping. But on the other hand, a good wife can be a definite asset and a bad one can be a downfall.

Your greatest influence is in the home. You can add to your husband's wealth by stretching the family budget with good buys, or wise investments. Of course, a man who has a happy family is truly wealthy. We are in a great position to create that happiness in our home.

It also applies at church. A man serving as deacon must have his household under control. If you are contentious, the church may and should think twice before asking your husband to serve on this board, even if he is the best qualified in all other aspects.

Other translations say:

> "Faith in her" (Bas) instead of "Trust her"
>
> > When you trust someone, you know you can depend on them. When you put your faith in someone, you are putting them on a higher level; you believe them to be something more. The difference may be slight, but it becomes great when you realize the focus has changed. It is no longer on the man, but is now on the woman. She has become greater than her

husband. Perhaps even greater than God. This ought not to be so.

instead of "He will have no need of spoil"

"She will not deprive him of the spoil" (SPRL); "gain he shall not lack" (RHM) or "He will never lack profit" (BER)

Again, the change in wording is slight, but now it sounds like he's going to be raking in the dough and she won't get any. Wouldn't that be kind of selfish of him not to share, when he is supposed to be providing? If he truly loved her and treated her as God told him to, he would be giving her the spoils of his labor.

But, do you really think God is talking about a lot of money coming into this marriage? I don't, I'm not saying it can't or won't happen, but I believe God places a much higher value on other things, and it is those things that he is talking about here. Such as the wife who will be such a blessing, he won't need riches. It is her value that is displacing his needs.

Discussion 3

She seeketh wool, and flax, and worketh willingly with her hands. Pro. 31:13

1. What is the significance (Characteristics) of wool and flax?

2. How can we apply the characteristics of wool & flax to ourselves?

3. Why is physical strength important for a wife? Isn't that supposed to be a man's character trait?

4. Where do we get inner strength?

5. As long as we do everything that's expected of us, is that enough? Why or why not?

6. What kind of attitude should you have?

CH 3

She seeketh wool, and, and worketh willingly with her hands. Pro. 31:13

Fun time is over. Time to start working. Time to go through the closets, dig out the sewing machine, get on your hands and knees; and scrub, scrub, scrub! Don't you wish you lived back in the time this was written? You could forget about washing the floors, since they were made of dirt anyway. (Or is that another misconception of the backward nature of our ancient ancestors? Remember the palaces Saul built?)

Make all your clothes by hand; an all but lost art now that the sewing machine has been invented. But then making your own clothes is an almost lost art, with all the ready-made clothes available.

Of course, we can't forget taking our laundry down to the local watering hole and beating them on the rocks. If it wasn't for that, and getting our drinking water from the town well, how would we ever have found the time to catch up on the local gossip?

Those days are gone. When you think of all the hardships you tend to say "good riddance!" But look, at all we've sacrificed, to get to where we are.

In many places you have to keep your door locked, even when you're home and up. You don't dare open it if there's someone on the other side you don't know. Even your best friend will turn on you for no apparent reason.

Yes, we have everything you could ever imagine; but, no time to enjoy it. A working definition of family now is; "A group of people sleeping in the same house; and not always at the same time." Many times, you don't even see each other for weeks. This ought not to be so.

Still, I believe we should make the best of what we have. So, let's see what that is. The first thing God did after creation, was to institute marriage. So, what better place is there to start?

Regardless of what science and man are trying to teach us, when God creates something, He creates it to last and to remain in the form He created it. (That's why when you mix a horse and donkey the creature it makes cannot reproduce.)

When God created man, He made him intelligent, strong, able to think and do things for himself. But he had one great need, companionship.

God noted that it was not good for man to be alone. He wasn't talking about man's need for Him, although that is a very real need in everyone's life. No, He was talking about something very different. This need could only be filled by the creation of woman.

Therefore, when God created woman, He made her different from man. She had to compliment him, not compete with him. So, He gave her the characteristics of wool – a warm, caring, loving, nurturing spirit for those around her, and of flax- inner strength, wrapped in a beautiful package. He intended this complete package of warmth, softness, strength, and beauty to last throughout all future generations.

So, now we've read five words, "She seeks wool and flex", and from two of these we have four areas to work on. Remember, they are already a part of us; we just need to bring them out.

Warmth: Cozy, loving, kind, giving:

Warmth involves a lot more than body temperature. It is your character and personality. Are you fun to be with, or do you drag everyone down, with your not so sweet disposition? Are you receptive and caring of others? Do you make people feel welcome when they come to your home or church, or do they want to run out the nearest door when they see you coming?

Warmth comes from within; it radiates out to those around. If you don't have that radiating warmth, it's time to work on getting it. But where does it come from? Years and years of soaking up the sunshine? No, that only gets you cancer. It takes time spent in the SONshine.

Remember, Jesus can do in one day what it takes others a thousand years to do, but you need to stay in His shine to keep it. (Also remember, this time He is working with us stubborn humans, so it may take a little longer to get it.)

A good place to start would be with a word study on the word "Love". If you've ever looked at a concordance you know there is page after page on the word "love", so plan on spending a couple of years on this. Look up two or three passages a day. Don't just read them, study them, ask God to reveal to you what he wants you to absorb from His Word.

As you study through those you should start getting a nice warm feeling, that will start spilling over and out onto those around you. Don't stop it, just let it naturally happen, and keep filling yourself with God's love so the over flow will never stop.

Softness:

Everyone talks about how soft a woman's skin is, and yes, it is important to do whatever you can to keep your skin soft and pleasing to the touch, for your husband. But, when God speaks of characteristics, He is usually speaking of the person within. A soft and gentle spirit is more likely what He had in mind here.

So, how do you acquire that soft and gentle spirit? Yes, I have to say it, so if you don't want to hear it, close your eyes. That's right, I said eyes. Since you're reading, you hear through your eyes. You acquire a soft and gentle spirit the same way you attain patience, through trials and tribulations.

Remember, while going through these, that, *a soft answer turns away wrath*. (Proverbs 15:1)

Begin with INTENSE prayer. Ask that this lesson be QUICKLY learned. Then do word studies on "Meekness", "Gentleness", "Self-control" Are these words sounding familiar to you? Yea, go ahead, study all the fruit, one section at a time. Remember, it is "fruit", not "fruits"; you can't have one without having all.

Galatians 5:22-23

But the fruit of the Spirit is love, joy, peace, longsuffering, gentleness, goodness, faith, Meekness, temperance: against such there is no law.

If you have love, you will have joy and be at peace. You will be kind, good and patient, faithful and gentle. If you have all of the above, you will have no need to blow up at anyone. If you lose your patience, you won't be very loving, kind or good. As for joy and self-control, they're out the window too.

Yes, the fruit does walk hand in hand. If you have one section, you have all the sections. Blow it in one, and you blow it in all. It is possible to walk in the Spirit one minute and be totally without Him the next. But, the more control you give Him, the longer He will be able to keep you.

Some would say that it's hard to have self-control when you really love someone, or something, like CHOCOLATE! But, when you're dealing with the fruit, that view HAS to be wrong. So, what is self-control?

> *"Effective command or control over one's own actions or emotions."*

Let's see, you see CHOCOLATE, you like CHOCOLATE, you reach for CHOCOLATE. Do you get yogurt instead? If not, then I guess your action was pretty well controlled; you got what you reached for. (Sorry, I couldn't resist.)

If we have love, joy, peace on a consistent basis, then we have our emotions under control. We usually tend to go over the deep end when our emotions are flared up. If they are flared, we probably don't have love joy and peace.

IT IS POSSIBLE TO WALK IN THE SPIRIT,

SO, WALK IN HIM.

Strength:

Jesus was a very misunderstood man, as I'm sure you've heard a million times, if you've been around church folk very long. Many would say He was weak, easily bullied; definitely not strong. But we know better, He was the strongest man that ever lived. No; not the strength of Samson, (although, He probably was stronger than Samson, even though He didn't feel the need to flex His muscles), but strength of character. He didn't back down from what was right, nor did He feel the need to defend Himself from false accusations.

He didn't need physical strength, he just had to say, fall down and they would. No one could touch Him if He didn't allow it.

Jesus had an inner strength, one we all need to tap into. When His disciples offered Him food at the well, He said, "I have food you know not of." (John 4:32) His food supply was His strength supply and that was prayer.

You may have noticed I talk a lot about prayer. That is because without a consistent communication with our Heavenly Father, you might as well throw this book away. There is no way possible for you to become a virtuous wife without Him.

Prayer is the lifeline we all need to survive. With it, we can accomplish anything, because God will be able to work through and in us. Without it, we're all alone, and doomed to failure.

Grab on to that line God is dangling in front of you and don't let go; get it as short as you can. He will make it as long as He needs to for you to reach, but when it is long, there is a lot of swaying. It is much harder to hold on to, a much bigger chance of you letting go and falling. Get it short, where you can get and keep a firm grip.

Beauty:

Some say that beauty is in the eye of the beholder but, is it? There are many beautiful women in the world made ugly by their attitudes and actions. There are plain women made beautiful by their loving concern for others.

We should all endeavor to be the most beautiful we can be for our husbands. This is not vanity, but rather a desire to be pleasing to them.

However, don't make the mistake of thinking that in order to accomplish this you need that thousand-dollar makeover. Beauty starts on the inside. When the inside is ugly all the money and makeup in the world isn't enough to make the outside beautiful. But, love in the heart can make the plainest face beautiful to the most critical eye.

I Peter 3:3-4

Whose adorning let it not be that outward adorning of plaiting the hair, and of wearing of gold, or of putting on of apparel; But let it be the hidden man of the heart, in that which is not corruptible, even the ornament of a meek and quiet spirit, which is in the sight of God of great price.

I Timothy 2:9

In like manner also, that women adorn themselves in modest apparel, with shamefacedness and sobriety; not with broided hair, or gold, or pearls, or costly array;

Does this mean we can't braid our hair, wear makeup, jewelry or nice clothing?

Shamefacedness suggests modesty, and or reverence to God. (Strongs #127).

Yes, these verses seem to be saying that we should not wear any of these things. But, a look through the Old Testament shows us that the Israelites wore all these things. Many references are made about the bride adorned for her groom. How God adorns His bride, Israel. And all these things are good. (Isaiah 61:10, Jeremiah 2:32, Ezekiel 16:7-14)

It isn't so much that God is against jewelry or costly clothing; but rather the flaunting of these things. He doesn't want us dressed in rags. Remember, the virtuous wife was dressed in scarlet and purple, symbolizing royalty.

But He also doesn't want us to give the air of being better than someone else. We are here as servants, not queens. We should be striving to show the beauty that is within us, not cover it over with a superficial showy outer beauty.

He's saying don't let your beauty be that outward showy beauty. These things are superficial and cannot create true beauty. Beauty should always come from inside.

We must also remember that Jewelry in Biblical days was worn for different reasons. Some were symbols of other gods, or had to do with the worship of other gods, and for that reason the Israelites was not to wear it.

So, what is the incorruptible ornament of a gentle and quiet spirit? (Definitions taken from Webster's 1828. Words in parenthesis are mine.)

Incorruptible:

Cannot be induced to act dishonestly. It is morally strong. Does not decay or become rotten.

Ornament:

That which embellishes; something which when added to another thing renders it more beautiful to the eye.

Grace:

Harmony or beauty of form, movement, or expression. Sense of propriety, consideration, freely given good well, beneficence, or mercy

Dignity:

Nobility of character or manner.

Luster:

Quality of shining by reflected light. (of the Son) Luminous glow, sheen, radiance, brightness.

Gentle:

Mild and kindly in manner, nature or tone. Not severe, rough, or loud. Soft, moderate, easily handled (by husband?), docile, tame, respectable, polite, refined.

Soft:

Easily yielding to touch or pressure. Tender, sympathetic, compassionate.

Polite:

Tactful consideration for others.

Quiet:

Little or no noise, little or no motion, still, free from excessive activity, turmoil, disturbance. Not showy, pretentious or brash.

All of these make up a beautiful spirit.

Yes, a woman should have outer beauty. It doesn't have to be the beauty of a model, but God wants everyone to be the best they can be. Remember, this kind of beauty truly is in the eye of the beholder and that inner beauty DOES affect it. Beauty is vain, but ugly drives everyone away. There is a fine line and we need to take care not to cross it on either side.

Now, to put it all together, (If you are reading this book in preparation for marriage, skip this until you have been married at least a month) read "Song of Solomon" every day for a month. Feel the warmth of their love, the softness of their touch, the gentleness of their strength, and the love of her beauty, his handsome features. Remember where they came from. It's not just the outward appearance, but the love from within for each other.

After the first week, start putting yourself and your husband in their place. Personalize it. At the end of the month, write your own "love story". Follow this outline, but put in events that apply to your life. Don't worry, I'm not going to ask you to share it with anyone, except your husband and I won't insist on that.

There is a devotional book based on The Song of Solomon, if you haven't already, now might be a good time to read it. It is *The Divine Romance by* Dr. Brian Simmons & Gretchen Rodriguez, published by Broadstreet Publishing.

Now, that we've gotten through the character-building part of this verse, it's time to start "Working with our hands!" No, I'm not going to "Spiritualize" or "Symbolize" this; I believe it means exactly what it says. Remember, a little hard work never hurt anyone.

Note, this does not say, "She works hard with her hands", but rather, "She WILLINGLY works with her hands." Attitude means a lot! Have you ever met a warm, soft, beautiful woman that was always complaining about all the work she had to do? Didn't think so. But, on the other hand I have met a lot of hard-working women who were warm, soft, beautiful, loving, kind and generous.

Now is the time to tackle that big house. Believe me, right now, a one-room studio apartment IS a big house. The best place to start is with a plan. This plan will change slightly, depending on the stage of life you are in.

- Stage one, newly married, no children. You just have you and your husband to worry about.

- Stage two, young children at home. A little more trying since you now have to put their needs ahead of the cleaning, it may take a lot longer to finish. Some find it much easier at this stage to take care of knick-knacks and excess things. Less breakage and less cleaning. Others use the excess as training grounds to train their children not to touch or to pick things up.

- Stage three older school age children at home. Depending on if they are going out to school, or if you are homeschooling this could create more time for you for spring cleaning or less, either way it is possible to set aside enough time every day for what needs to be done.

- Stage four empty nest syndrome. Back to just you and your husband. Time to re-evaluate This is one of the times many couples break up, they can't make the adjustments, or more accurately, won't make the adjustments. This could be one of the best times of your marriage, but you have to work at making it so. Take the time to get to know each other again and spend time doing things you both enjoy together. But that is another topic in this book. Today we are talking about cleaning, so let's get back to it.

This is only an example; you'll need to find one that works for you. Remember, different stages of your life require different plans and time tables.

I started when my children were ages 1,2,4, & 9. At that time, I had let my prayer and devotional life slip. So, my first priority was to get that back on schedule. That in itself was a struggle, with four young children at home. There's always something needing to be done and satan takes full advantage. Every time I'd try to pray, someone got into something. If I got up early, they'd get up too.

Then, God stepped in and gave me the time I needed, through two very special people. A friend called one day and said God had told her I needed to rest, so she and another friend wanted to help. They would take my children for two hours a day for two weeks.

I didn't know how to respond at first. I wanted to scream out, (First clue I really needed the break) "I'm fine! I don't need rest! I can handle it! God wouldn't have given me four children and told me to Homeschool if I couldn't handle it." But I also knew she wouldn't call and tell me God told her I did, if she wasn't sure that God had said it.

I said thank-you, and we made our plans for the next two weeks. After dropping the children off the first day I went home and prayed. I said, "Lord, I don't feel right about this, but if this is what you want, show me what I'm supposed to do with this time."

To make a long story short, I had one hour of uninterrupted prayer every day. The Lord gave me plans for the immediate future, an outline to follow for the summer, answers to questions that had been bugging me for a long time and taught me to rest in Him.

My second week of time I spent on nights alone with my husband. We went out to supper one night and supper alone at home another. But my hour of prayer each day, continued. I allowed the children to watch one video movie in the morning and that was my prayer time.

I've struggled with that hour through the years, slipping many times, usually due to getting up too late. But I am determined God will be (is) the victor; satan will not win this battle.

Although, now in my fourth stage of life I have found that I really allowed it to slip through the years, that hour has decreased to fifteen minutes. Time to get back on track; as I feel the loss in other areas of my life as well.

Following is my "ideal" schedule. Keep in mind, each stage of life produces its own struggles and it will be hard to stay on schedule. Also, be it understood that time with husband, or doing things he asks for, overrules the schedule at any time. Also, bear in mind, this is a general schedule.

Some days change with special events like: Church activities, school meetings, field trips, park days, 4-H, doctor appointments and numerous other events.

I've always wanted to get up before the sun and do my devotions outside while watching the sun come up. When my children were young, I found that to be impossible. No matter what time I went to bed, I just couldn't seem to get up before 7. God let me know that it was okay not to be an early riser. Instead, I stayed up late and got much more done than I could by getting up earlier.

It wasn't until my children were grown and gone, and I was into my second marriage that I have managed to occasionally get up before the sun. My husband goes to bed earlier so I do too, most nights. My days are more my own so I get the things done then, that I used to do at night.

I had been trying to write a book for ten years, and couldn't find the time to work on it. When the Lord told me to do it at night, I got five times as much done the first month as I had in the last ten years. That was when the children were young. I had three books almost finished and two more started.

Being I do much better on four hours sleep than I do on eight, I used to stay up until two or three in the morning and sleep until 7 or 8. Being I homeschooled, I could let the children stay up late so they would sleep later (maybe).

Not only did they not get up and run around at 6:30, but they got to spend a little more time with daddy. My husband got up early for work and didn't want to get up any earlier for breakfast. If he did, I would have gotten up by 5 to make it.

Now, onto the schedule: (This is my schedule when the kids were young. Adjust the times to fit you)

7:00 a.m.	Get up/Personal Devotions/Pray
8:30	Breakfast/Devotions with Children
9:30	House Cleaning
12:30	Lunch
1:30	Naps/School
5:00	Supper

Evening	Family Time
7/9	Children's bed times
10:00	Book Writing

As the children got older, many things changed. School time started in the morning, and extended to the afternoon. Years later, and marriage number 2 much changed.

After the children left home, I got a job and worked overnights for over 10 years, when that got to be too much, I switched to 2nd shift for another 4 years before finally being able to come home again. We now work with special needs and have someone living with us.

During my working outside the home years, I was lucky if I got 3 hours sleep at one time. But God saw me through. Although I am sure that was not the ideal or what God really wanted, I know He saw me through because of my submission to my husband.

Sometimes it was touch and go. There were many times I wanted to say I know better and I'm not doing this. But I did know better and knew my husband had the final say rather I agreed with it or not. But all in all, the last 18 years have been good years.

During that time, I stopped writing. Just didn't have the time for it. I missed it and I had many internal struggles, knowing that was what I should be doing. Even after coming home, it took a year or two to get back into writing. I was starting to think it was lost for good. But again, God saw me through that time.

My new husband is a Christian. Newly saved when we met, and has had a lot of struggles through the years, but is committed and looking to live as God wants. We don't always agree on what that is, but we will get there.

Now, to break it down a little more, my cleaning schedule is as follows: (Again when the children were young.)

Sun. Morning Church

Afternoon Work in Garden (Living in the south at the time that was a year-round thing.)

Mon. Master Bed & bath; ½ bath; Laundry room; wash downstairs floors; 1-2 loads of laundry.

Tue. Women's Bible Study (Church); laundry

Wed. Living room; Den; Kitchen; laundry

Thurs. Check upstairs (Children are responsible for their own rooms & upstairs bath); finish cleaning anything that didn't get done during the week; laundry

Fri. Preparation day- Cook for Saturday (No, I'm not Jewish, nor a Seventh-day Adventist, but I do believe the fourth Commandment means exactly what it says.); Haircuts as needed; laundry

Sat. Sabbath day of rest as outlined in Ex. 20. (Out of love for God, not by letter of the law.)

Even though I've spread the cleaning out over four days it can be done in two or three, once you get the spring cleaning done. (To be discussed in a few minutes.) And, yes, with four children I really did, do laundry almost every day.

Some weeks this too changed, due to other events as mentioned earlier. No schedule is perfect, nor can it account for everything. We have to be flexible; but I find most people do need a schedule or they don't get anything done. I happen to be one of those people. Don't be afraid to plan and don't hesitate to change those plans. Allow God to be in control.

Over the years this changed some too. We didn't have a garden as the kids got older so Sunday became my heavy cleaning day. During the week I tried to keep the house picked up, working between helping the children with their studies, etc. The children also had a little more responsibility.

2nd marriage...With just the two of us at home the cleaning schedule became much lighter, now that we have a third it's still pretty light but life is definitely different. I now do a lot of my writing during the day, and evenings are spent relaxing before bed. I actually get seven to eight hours sleep, most nights; and still manage to get up between five and six a.m.

How do you make a schedule and keep to it? First rule; don't plan too much at first. It is probably best to get into a routine. Start with one room. Clean everything visible and straighten it up. When finished move on to the next room.

Don't worry about getting everything. This time through is just to get the surface stuff and get your routine started. If it takes two weeks this first time through, that's okay, but try to do it in one. The idea is to have a clean house, not a perfect one. (Don't worry about the windows this time, unless they're so bad you can't see out of them.)

Repeat the above until you are comfortably getting through the whole house in a week without spending all day on it. Be sure to do something fun every day. Don't forget your family.

They need a happy mom more than a spotless house. SPEND TIME WITH THEM!

Second step: Now, the fun begins! This is the step I call spring-cleaning, even if it's summer, fall or winter. Pick one room for your special weekly task. (I like starting at one end of the house and working my way through. If there are two stories, I start upstairs.) Do your normal cleaning each day then spend an hour or two in that room. Clean it from top to bottom, including windows, ceiling and walls this time.

Get rid of anything you don't need. Clean out your closets. If it doesn't belong in that room, or fit the theme of that room, but you want to keep it, put it somewhere else. (Preferably in the room you want it in, you don't want to get trapped into moving it from room to room. But, if there isn't room for it there yet, find a temporary place for it.)

Get that room organized BEFORE moving on. Don't allow yourself to be sidetracked when moving something to another room.

When you finish, whether it takes a day or three weeks, take a day off, do something special with the family; than tackle the next room. Keep going till you finish the whole house. You may want to start with the basement so you will have a place to put everything you don't want.

When you finish, have a yard sale or give everything to someone who can USE them, or to a worthwhile charity. (Of course, if it is trash throw it away, non-profits get enough trash, they don't need yours.)

Some will say mend and or repair as you go. Others say set it aside and do it later. I would say that depends on what it is.

If it is something you need to finish what you're working on, by all means get it fixed. On the other hand, you should have some time set aside each week for mending and repairing. So, you could put it in the room you do that stuff in and it will be waiting for you at the appropriate time.

If mending and sewing are not your things, there's nothing here that says you have to do it yourself. There's a great little system that has been developed through the years. Used correctly, it can be a big help. It's called "bartering".

Find someone who likes to sew and let them do yours in exchange for something you enjoy doing that they don't like. (Perhaps you could baby-sit or make them a special meal or dessert. Maybe do a special craft item, or help them with a big project at their home.)

When you finish your spring-cleaning, if done effectively, you should be able to cut your cleaning time in half. Unless, your house was already completely organized and clutter free. Do something really special, you've worked really hard and deserve it.

When I started, our garage was so full of boxes there was a six-inch zigzag path, maybe. I spent the first month going through boxes. I threw out about eight boxes of junk, gave another ten to fifteen boxes to our church for a yard sale, brought some things into the house and repacked the rest.

My husband obtained enough room to work out there and built a cabinet for the pool supplies. Needless to say, he was very surprised and happy to see the garage floor for the first time in over six months.

If you need more help determining what to keep and what to throw, these books may help:

"Clutters Last Stand" by, Don Asletts

"Is There Life After Housework?" by Don Asletts

Other translations say:

Instead of "Works willingly with her hands"

"Diligent hands" (SPRL)

"Plying her hands with ready skill" (KNOX)

> You can be diligent at a task and not be doing it willingly. I think this Scripture is talking as much about attitude as it is about getting the work done.

"And works it up as she wills" (AAT)

> Very head strong woman? I don't think so.

"And toils at her work" (NEB)

> Sounds like she's being forced, not working willingly.

Discussion 4

She is like the merchants' ships; she bringeth her food from afar. She riseth also while it is yet night, and giveth meat to her household, and a portion to her maidens. Prov. 31:14-15

1. How should we be shopping for food today?

2. Is it necessary to get up early and make a good breakfast for the family, before they go off to work and school?

3. Is this section dealing only with food for the body?

4. So, what should a family breakfast include?

CH 4

She is like the merchants' ships; she bringeth her food from afar. She riseth also while it is yet night, and giveth meat to her household, and a portion to her maidens. Prov. 31:14-15

Does this mean she was not a gardener, or a "farmer's wife"? Probably not, back in the days this was written, most lived off the land. Their crops and animals determined their wealth. Granted, slaves or hired servants, for many, did most of the work, but food for the household still came from their own crops.

So, what is meant by "She bringeth her food from afar"? Many women in those days were gleaners in the fields. Sometimes, they would have to walk many miles to find a field to glean. But, if they were poor or widowed, that is what they had to do. Even their own fields could be a long way from the home.

No, I'm not saying you have to stop going to the store and plant a garden, although, it would be better for you and your family. Garden fresh, grown without chemicals, is much healthier and nutritious, (tastes better too). The fewer preservatives, the better the flavor and nutritional value. Remember, "enriched" on the label means: God-made natural vitamins and minerals have been taken out, man-made synthetic vitamins and minerals have been added. (Not very enriching to my way of thinking.)

Merchant ships bring goods in from all over the known world, thereby giving their customers the best selection possible. Likewise, a virtuous wife should have a wide variety of foods available to her family. In order to have a well-balanced nutritional diet you need a variety of foods. This will supply all the essential vitamins and minerals and also keep your family from getting bored with the same old thing.

The Biblical definition of day is "sunrise to sunset". Therefore, sunset to sunrise was night. (Gen. 1:5 God called the darkness night and the light day.) So, to rise while it is yet night simply means before sunrise.

I am reminded of something else here I need to mention. Hope I don't confuse you too badly. The Sabbath starts at

Sunset on Friday and goes until Sunset on Saturday. A full twenty-four-hour period. So, sunset starts the new day, but it is also night.

With only candlelight to see by at night you couldn't do much, so, you had to make good use of the day light hours. The men were up and out early tending to the flocks, herds and fields. A good wife and mother would never allow them to leave without a good meal in their stomach and lots of food in their pack. In order to do this, she would have to be up way before the sun.

I can hear the moaning and complaining already. "Not only does she want us to tend a garden but now she wants us to get up before dawn and make a big breakfast!" A virtuous wife would never moan and complain. We'll have to work on that one.

In reality, our life is so different. For some who work the night shift they're just getting to bed when the sun is coming up. So, no, this is not the time for a big breakfast. But, for us more "traditional" types; who have children going to school and a husband that leaves by seven A.M., breakfast is still the most important meal of the day. Yes, you may have to get up early to fix it and if you are going off to work yourself, that makes it even earlier.

So, do you really have to eat a big breakfast? Some say breakfast is the most essential meal of the day, other's say 'eating as soon as I get up makes me sick'. Some eat just fruit; others ham and eggs. Your breakfast, and the time you eat it, should be what is right and best for you.

If you follow the Body Type diet, you will find that different body types, need to eat different foods at different times, for their body to make the best use of it. Some need to eat within the first half hour of getting up; others need to wait two to three hours before eating. Some need six to eight small meals a day, others two to three larger meals. There is no one size fits all diet.

Now, we come to the part we all like, MAIDSERVANTS! Can we really have maids? Yes, maybe not the way you're thinking right now, but with a little creativity, anything can be accomplished. As we have need, God will provide. BUT that doesn't mean you can get lazy! A virtuous wife is NEVER lazy! She must stay on top of everything and everyone under her control. She is perhaps the busiest one in the household.

OOPS! Sorry. I was looking at the NEW King James. It says, "She provides food for her household, and a portion for her maidservants." But, getting back to the OLD King James, we find that it simply says "Maidens", which means: "a girl from infancy to adolescence." This verse could be referring to her daughters. It could be talking about servant girls, but we need to be careful about making assumptions. Besides, wouldn't the servants be providing the meals for you? We don't really know if she had servants or not.

This we do know, the inspiration of this scripture was most likely the first one up, and the last one to bed, with very few breaks in between. She was very organized, kept up with her husband and children's schedules, as well as her own and everyone else in the household. She kept up with everything that needed to be done and never complained.

She was not only an inspiration to Saul, the writer of this section of Proverbs, whom many believe to be her son, but she is also an inspiration to us. We do not have to envy her or hate her, for she has shown us a better way. One we CAN follow and find life much more enjoyable, by doing so.

Yes, we do need to face reality. Not too many of us have servants or maids. Rather this scripture is really talking about them or not, there is one thing we can glean from this possibility. We don't have to do everything ourselves. We can delegate some of the responsibility to others. Children, even little ones, can handle some tasks.

By the time a child can walk, he can carry his toys. If he can carry his toys, he can take care of them too. He can also pick up other small items and take care of them. This is a good time to teach colors, shapes and numbers.

"Tommy could you pick up the two square blocks and put them in the red bucket please." "Thank-you, that was so good." "Sara, could you put the blue bowl in the sink, please." Don't forget to say please and thank-you. Praise them for a job well done. This is a great time to teach manners as well.

Older children would need less direct contact. "Sally, would you sweep the floors for me please." Remember, if you want your children to be respectful and well mannered, you need to treat them with respect, and show those same good manners.

Next, comes the things you hate, and nobody else in your family can do. That's where the bartering system comes in. You find someone who can and offer to do something else for them in exchange. By trading your talents, no money changes hands and that dreaded task gets done.

If all else fails and you have some extra money, as long as it's acceptable to your husband, you can hire a maid. It doesn't have to be full time, just whenever you need one; one time only, once a week, or once a month.

You don't have to stick to normal household chores. You buy what you need. Today you can find someone to do almost anything from shopping to washing the dog. The day they figure out how to get someone to exercise for you and you get the benefit; I'm sure a lot will be signed up for the service.

Other translations say:

"She buys imported food, brought by ship from distant ports." (TAY)

> I can't see a lot of people buying food in those days. They grew what they needed. Besides, with no preservatives, fresh food wouldn't survive those long voyages. Remember, the text says, "She is like..." it didn't say she actually bought anything.

She gives food to her household and work to her maids (LAM, JERUS, & TAY) (All three say this slightly different)

> Those poor maids, can't they eat too? So many translations said this that I looked up "portion" and traced it back to the Hebrew. This word means: *an enactment hence an appointment (of time, space, quantity, labor, or usage); appointed, bound, commandment, convenient, custom, decree, due, law, measure, x necessary, ordinance, (nary), portion, set time, statute, task.*

Of course, when you think about it, the maids or more correctly, maidens were part of the household. So, everyone got fed, then the men and boys went to the fields; the girls stayed home and helped with the chores. It was up to mom to divide out the work for the day.

Discussion 5

She considereth a field, and buyeth it: with the fruit of her hands she planteth a vineyard. She girdeth her loins with strength, and strengtheneth her arms. She perceiveth that her merchandise is good: her candle goeth not out by night. She layeth her hands to the spindle, and her hands hold the distaff. Pro. 31:16-19

1. What is today's field to buy and plant?
2. What kind of fruit would you grow in your vineyard?
3. In evaluating your abilities used in your field, what questions should you ask yourself?
4. What other kind of vineyard could she be planting?
5. Is it necessary to plan a daily exercise program?
6. If your light does not go out by night, does that mean you should be a workaholic; working all day and night? Or that you should sleep all day so you can stay up all night?

CH 5

She considereth a field, and buyeth it: with the fruit of her hands she planteth a vineyard. She girdeth her loins with strength, and strengtheneth her arms. She perceiveth that her merchandise is good: her candle goeth not out by night. She layeth her hands to the spindle, and her hands hold the distaff. Pro. 31:16-19

This is my favorite part of this piece of scripture. I dreamed about my "field" for years. It wasn't until well into my second marriage that I got it. About 30 years after starting this book,

I got my field! We now own 58 acres. After living here for 7 years I finally got to stay home and enjoy it. Three years later we started some of the work we've been wanting to do. Hoping to get a lot more done over the next couple of years and maybe soon get a Chicken house built so we can get chickens the following spring.

I always wanted to go back to a simpler time where family was still a family, with dad working at, or near home; where the children could spend time with him. Helping in the fields, barn, or at the family business. They learn more from life than they ever could from books. (That doesn't mean I don't believe in schooling. I certainly do. Books are important and when used correctly, we need to use more of them.)

This, to most sounds like a far-fetched dream that will never come true. Believe what you want, but one day I will have that and more. This has been a desire of mine for a long time and God promises us the desires of our heart, IF we love Him AND are called according to His purpose. Besides, I know He gave me this desire.

For me it is a literal field, but it doesn't have to be that for you. For a better understanding on this, see my answers to Discussion 5 questions 1-3. Now, let's go see what Webster's has to say about "Field":

> 1. Piece of land, usually covered with vegetation (Not a garden) and having few or no trees or structures.
>
> 9. Range of interest; particular division or sphere of activity. Sphere of particular activity, as in research or business, away from the laboratory or home office.

As the Webster's 1828 dictionary points out; In the Bible, Field usually means a large area of land a good way away from the home.

While you are considering what and where your field is, perhaps you should also consider:

God's plan for woman

Titus 2:3-5

The aged women likewise, that they be in behaviour as becometh holiness, not false accusers, not given to much wine, teachers of good things; That they may teach the young women to be sober, to love their husbands, to love their children, To be discreet, chaste, keepers at home, good, obedient to their own husbands, that the word of God be not blasphemed.

The original Greek word for "keepers" is "oikouros" (Strongs 3626) which means "a stayer at home i/e domestically inclined (a "good housekeeper"): - keeper at home." Now, with this in mind, PRAY, and be open to the Lord's guidance, as you determine what and where your field is.

While we're on this topic, let's take a few minutes to discuss the wife's role in the home and church. To help us understand more fully, what our role is, we will take a look at Scriptures dealing with this topic. First, the Creation of Woman:

Genesis 2:18-23

And the Lord God said, It is not good that the man should be alone; I will make him an help meet for him. And out of the ground the Lord God formed every

beast of the field, and every fowl of the air; and brought them unto Adam to see what he would call them: and whatsoever Adam called every living creature, that was the name thereof. And Adam gave names to all cattle, and to the fowl of the air, and to every beast of the field; but for Adam there was not found an help meet for him. And the Lord God caused a deep sleep to fall upon Adam, and he slept: and he took one of his ribs, and closed up the flesh instead thereof; And the rib, which the Lord God had taken from man, made he a woman, and brought her unto the man. And Adam said, This is now bone of my bones, and flesh of my flesh: she shall be called Woman, because she was taken out of Man.

Notice, right from the start, God's creation of man was different from that of the animals. (Also notice, I did not say OTHER animals. Despite what many try to tell us, man is not an animal. Man has been given an intelligence that was not given to the animals, although many choose not to use it.)

Up to this point God made everything by speaking the Word. Male and Female animals were all made the same at the same time. But, here, He had already made Adam from the dust of the earth and seeing that he needed a help meet, (aid or helper) God made Women from his side.

Even though the King James says, "one of his ribs", the original reading would seem to imply that side would be a more accurate translation. Also, notice Adam says, "She is bone of my bones and Flesh of my flesh". Why would he say that if it was only one rib bone used in her making?

It would appear, as we talked about in an earlier chapter, that God used Adam's whole side to make Eve. So, she truly was a BIG part of him.

Why this difference? Because man's purpose was different. One of these purposes was to service the earth, take care of the animals and the rest of God's creation. Woman was created to serve man; to be a helper to him.

Woman was not taken from just anywhere. God took her from just the right spot. Not from Adam's head, so she would have all the brains and be superior to him, nor from his foot to be walked on and treaded under. She wasn't taken from his finger given her an extra hand with which to work.

No, she was taken from Adam's side, including ribs, which protect his most precious organs. Not only is she to serve him, but he is to protect her. She was to be to him, a most important part of himself. She was taken from his side, to walk beside him, not ahead or behind, but beside; to be his partner.

This is very symbolic of this special relationship. They are joined together, they are one. Neither is complete without the other. Perhaps, that is why it takes a man and a woman to make a marriage. How can two men or two women become one? The man and woman are one, because Adam gave part of himself to Eve; man to woman. Therefore, woman completes man in a way two women or two men never could.

You know the Bible doesn't tell us which side God used to make women, but I think it was the left side, because the left brain controls the artistic tendencies and the right controls the physical action, problem solving. Men tend to be more "this is how to do it, get it done"; while women tend to find more creative solutions to the problems. (I know, I know the left brain controls the right side, but remember, she got the whole side, including that side of the brain, so it would have to be left side.) ☺

Genesis 3:16

Unto the woman he said, I will greatly multiply thy sorrow and thy conception; in sorrow thou shalt bring forth children; and thy desire shall be to thy husband, and he shall rule over thee.

This so-called curse on woman is actually one of the greatest blessings God could ever give us. The pain in childbirth we could gladly do without. I tend to think that is the curse and the later part of this verse is just setting things in order. Getting them back where they were meant to be, for that was most surely Heaven sent, with love.

Our desire *SHALL* be for our husband. RIGHT WHERE IT SHOULD BE! Just as God intended from the beginning. Remember, He made Eve from Adam's side, as his HELP MEET (Gen. 2:18), to *fit in* with him, to *fill in* where he was lacking. NOT to take control, but to help where and when needed.

"And he shall rule over you" His rule is one of love and protection. As the rib, which he sacrificed for you would imply. Even though God used his whole side, we know woman has one more rib than man does, so it would appear he sacrificed a rib, since it was not replaced with new as the rest of his side was.

This in no way gives him permission to abuse you in any way, mentally, emotionally or physically. When this happens, he is not showing love nor exercising his God given authority as head of household. And he most certainly is not protecting you. God has NOT called any to live in this manner.

I Peter 3:7

Likewise, ye husbands, dwell with them according to knowledge, giving honour unto the wife, as unto the weaker vessel, and as being heirs together of the grace of life; that your prayers be not hindered.

"The weaker vessel"? Yes, this is a verse a lot of women would like to throw out, sorry; I'm not one of them. Like it or not, women are the weaker vessel. But that is not a bad thing, it is just stating a fact.

Physically, women are weaker than men. Yes, a woman can work out and increase her strength and there are some women that are stronger than some men, but over all this is not the case.

Notice that if a husband does not honor his wife, treat her right, his prayers are hindered. Why do you think that is? Perhaps, because by treating her badly he is sinning and sin separates you from God.

Colossians 3:19

Husbands, love your wives, and be not bitter against them.

Ephesians 5:25-33

Husbands, love your wives, even as Christ also loved the church, and gave himself for it; That he might

sanctify and cleanse it with the washing of water by the word, That he might present it to himself a glorious church, not having spot, or wrinkle, or any such thing; but that it should be holy and without blemish. So ought men to love their wives as their own bodies. He that loveth his wife loveth himself. For no man ever yet hated his own flesh; but nourisheth and cherisheth it, even as the Lord the church: For we are members of his body, of his flesh, and of his bones. For this cause shall a man leave his father and mother, and shall be joined unto his wife, and they two shall be one flesh. This is a great mystery: but I speak concerning Christ and the church. Nevertheless let every one of you in particular so love his wife even as himself; and the wife see that she reverence her husband.

Ah, yes, 'Husbands love your wives.' Why do you think God had to tell the men this so many times? Maybe because we need to be reminded so many times that they do truly love us.

It's so easy to get caught up in the day to day that we forget we are not in this life alone. Women have a deep-seated need to be loved and cherished. Yes, men need it too, but women need to be reminded more often. At least most do.

Personally, I cringe when my husband tells me he loves me. Not because of him, I know he means it, but because of my past. When my first husband said 'I love you' I thought, 'yeah, sure you do.' For him it was only words, his actions said he didn't care about me at all. Now, almost 20 years later, they are still just empty words that mean nothing.

Although my present husband doesn't just say it, he means it and shows me every day how much he loves me. I still can't accept the words and have a hard time saying them back to him. He knows I love him; I show him in other ways, but I also know he would like to hear it more often. Something I'm trying to work on even now.

"One flesh" is a concept often forgotten in marriages today. One we need to remember. It is no longer two people living together, compromising. It is not a 50/50 union. It is ONE person in two bodies giving 100%. Marriage should never be about what I can get, but rather, what I can give. It is not about what I want; it is about what we want together.

When following God's order and submitting *ourselves* to His rule, the rule of our husband is a glorious thing. Our husbands are a true covering of protection for us. We are greatly blessed.

I believe one of the reasons for the fall was that Adam did not take his rightful place. During all the time the serpent was talking with Eve, Adam was right there, listening, yet he never said a word.

What was he thinking? Why didn't he speak up? We don't know, but, perhaps, if he had taken his protective position at this time, Eve would never have bitten the forbidden fruit, and we would still have access to that beautiful garden today. Instead, he stood back and let Eve talk with the serpent. He let her make the first move.

Perhaps, he was looking at the fruit, wondering what made it so different. Why would God say not to eat of it? Then, before he realized it, Eve was putting something into his hands saying, "Here, try this, it's soooo good."

Because Adam hesitated, Eve stepped in and took control. Women are still doing that today. God has said that man is to be the leader in the Church and in the home. Women are to be in submission to their own husband. Yet, the men hesitate to take their rightful, God-given place and women rush in to fill the gap.

Now, I know there are many that would disagree with me on that point. I have finally just heard an excellent teaching that almost has me convinced to change my mind; almost...but not quite. That teaching is discussed in one of the mini studies we read in a previous chapter.

I Timothy 2:11-3:5

Let the woman learn in silence with all subjection. But I suffer not a woman to teach, nor to usurp authority over the man, but to be in silence. For Adam was first formed, then Eve. And Adam was not deceived, but the woman being deceived was in the transgression. Notwithstanding she shall be saved in childbearing, if they continue in faith and charity and holiness with sobriety. This is a true saying, If a man desire the office of a bishop, he desireth a good work. A bishop then must be blameless, the husband of one wife, vigilant, sober, of good behaviour, given to hospitality, apt to teach; Not given to wine, no striker, not greedy of filthy lucre; but patient, not a brawler, not covetous; One that ruleth well his own house, having his children in subjection with all gravity; (For if a man know not how to rule his own house, how shall he take care of the church of God?)

Verses 11 & 12, are verses a lot of people don't know what to do with. They would like to take them out, rip them into very fine pieces and throw them away, or better yet, burn them. Of course, it's just your luck, I don't happen to be one of those people. I happen to like them and agree with them. So, let's take a closer look.

"Let the women learn in silence." Have you ever tried to learn something while you were talking? (Some women can, but it is very distracting for the men. ☺) You tend to miss the key words that bring everything into the light.

I've heard the teaching so many times that when this was written the women sat on one side of the church and the men on the other. According to this theory, the "Severely uneducated" women didn't know what the Rabbi was talking about so would holler over to her husband and ask him what he meant.

Guess it's been forgotten that back then, most of the educating was done at home, by the women. And what would they do with Debra, many hundreds of years earlier, even more severely uneducated? Then there's Priscilla, who worked alongside of her husband. Lois, Timothy's grandmother and his mother, and the list goes on. (In case you didn't figure it out, I don't think that is what this is talking about.)

Another reason I find this scenario unlikely, is that if a women did this, she would disgrace her husband. Not to mention get a lot of dirty looks from the other men and women. Yes, it is possible some of that was going on, hence the companion scripture: (Underline mine)

I Corinthians 14:34-38

Let your women keep silence in the churches: for it is not permitted unto them to speak; but they are commanded to be under obedience, as also saith the law. <u>And if they will learn any thing, let them ask their husbands at home</u>: for it is a shame for women to speak in the church. What? came the word of God out from you? or came it unto you only? If any man think himself to be a prophet, or spiritual, let him acknowledge that the things that I write unto you are the commandments of the Lord. But if any man be ignorant, let him be ignorant.

Speak here could mean preach, which makes a little more sense. When you talk of someone speaking in church you usually mean they went up front giving a message. And there were many women rising up at this time that had been with Jesus and heard the same things first hand that the Apostles heard. Wouldn't they have been equally knowledgeable and able to preach?

"Under obedience" means "in subjection, submit self unto." You can be in submission and still talk, but it is hard to be under submission, of anyone but God, when you are preaching. The preacher has to be in command of the situation. (Of course, there is the argument that a guest speaker is under the Pastor's authority, because he has given them permission to speak in his congregation.)

The next line shows that this is not a time for questions and answers. If a woman doesn't understand something, she should wait and ask her husband what was meant when they get home, rather than tying up everyone's time at church.

One last thought on this Scripture. There is a theory, as we talked about in an earlier chapter, that Paul was answering a concern that the Corinthians had, and that it was the men of the church that said women could not speak in Church. But, Paul was saying this isn't so.

His comment: "What? came the word of God out from you? or came it unto you only? If any man think himself to be a prophet, or spiritual, let him acknowledge that the things that I write unto you are the commandments of the Lord. But if any man be ignorant, let him be ignorant", would tend to make more sense.

Now, back to I Timothy; "I suffer not a woman to teach, nor to usurp authority over the man, but to be in silence." To usurp authority means "to seize and hold in possession by force."

Many women will say, "I'm not forcing any man to stay and listen to me; therefore, I'm not usurping authority and it's okay for me to teach or preach." But, if you go on, the rest of the definition says, "Or without right." These two scriptures hint at the fact that maybe we don't have the right.

I know I'm stepping on a lot of toes here and I hate to do that. I've heard a lot of good women preachers, (I use that term loosely because most of them were not ordained preachers). They researched their messages and presented the word accurately, many times better than some men I've heard.

So, I searched the Scripture and other sources trying to find where I had interpreted this wrong. I found a paper entitled "A Woman to Teach". I do not know who wrote it but it was well written and almost convinced me, until I checked out the facts. So, let's take a closer look.

This paper brought out the fact that Aquila and Priscilla took Apollos aside and "explained the way of God more accurately to Him." It told how Paul acknowledged several women as being co-workers. Very accurate, but does it say that any of them taught men?

Priscilla came close with Apollos, but she was working **with** her husband, I believe he took the lead in the conversation. Although some will say she was the lead because she was mentioned first. Maybe so, but many times in our culture when a man and his wife are introduced, the woman's name is mentioned first, other times the man's is. I don't know about the Hebrew custom.

This was one on one, not in a church setting. Although I believe they did have a home church and it appears both were leading it. Many feel that she could have been the leader of it, but the scripture doesn't tell us that.

She most likely had a lot of good insights to add to what her husband was saying and was most likely a great help to Apollos in understanding the scriptures. I am not trying to say that a woman cannot explain things to a man who is searching and asking, but it is not her place to teach men in a Church setting.

He then goes on to explain that "women" in I Timothy 2:8-14 is from the Greek word "Gune", which translates as "Married women" therefore, this scripture is talking about teaching your husband." Okay, I can kind of see that, but when checking this out I found that the word is from the Strong's reference #1135 Gune, which as this paper said means a woman; spec. a wife: - wife, women.

Okay, I was willing to give the writer that, until I looked at other New Testament verses that had the word women and found all but three came from the same root word. Those three were "Aged Women" "free women" and the third is "female, women" But the one I found most interesting was I Cor. 7:34 "The unmarried woman..." comes from the same root word, 1135- gune" although this paper says it comes from the word "Agamos" #22 which means: unmarried. The Strong's concordance references it under #1135. {Man in this scripture comes from #435 – "aner" meaning a man (prop. As an individual male): - fellow, husband, man, sir.}

Next the writer brings up the word "Quiet" in 1 Peter 3:1-5 as being the same word as Silence in I Tim. 2:11-12 saying that it is the Greek word "Hesuchios" meaning quiet in the sense of settled, steadfast, immovable. And says this is referring to a woman being settled and secure in her role as wife.

According to the Strongs the I Tim reference comes from #2270 "hesuchazo" meaning to keep still refrain from labor, meddlesomeness or speech:-cease, hold peace, be quiet, rest. from the same as #2272 which is the word in I Pet. 3:4 "hesuchios" meaning keeping one's seat (sedentary) i/e (by impl) still (undisturbed, undisturbing);-peaceable, quiet. And I Tim. 2:2 comes from #2263"eremos" meaning: (through the idea of stillness) tranquil:-quiet.

Silence, in I Cor. 14:28 & 34 comes from # 4601 "sigao" meaning to keep silent, keep close (secret, silence) hold peace. And I Tim. 2:11 & 12 comes from #2271 "hesuchia" meaning stillness, i/e desistance from bustle or language:- quietness, silence.

The writer also makes the comment "If we were to take the I Corinthians scripture to its logical conclusion, you could not allow any women teachers in Sunday School or nursery. Neither could they pray or sing."

Let's see, does it say that? The word Speak here comes from #2980 "laleo" meaning: to talk, utter words, preach, say, speak (after) talk, tell, utter. This tells us to compare #3004 which says that this word (#2980) means an extended or random harangue. I had not heard this word before so I looked up synonyms for it, they are: berate, lecture, criticize, rant, address, sermonize, scold, tirade. I don't see anything here that says they can't pray or sing.

As for teaching Sunday School or working in the nursery. I may be wrong, but I do not believe they had Sunday School or nursery in those days. The children remained with their mothers during the church service. Therefore, we cannot apply this scripture to our modern-day Sunday School or nursery. This topic was not addressed. BUT we do know that for the most part, the mothers taught their own children.

So, would this writer's conclusion be the logical one? Or, is he/she grasping at straws to make a point? Hate to say it, but I still don't see where this gives a woman permission to teach men.

BUT, if the thought that Paul was addressing a misconception of the Corinthian Church is right, then this could all be a lot of supposing for nothing, because Paul is not saying what we all thought he was. He was actually saying that women can speak in church.

Titus 2:1-5

But speak thou the things which become sound doctrine: That the aged men be sober, grave, temperate, sound in faith, in charity, in patience. The aged women likewise, that they be in behaviour as becometh holiness, not false accusers, not given to much wine, teachers of good things; That they may teach the young women to be sober, to love their husbands, to love their children, To be discreet, chaste, keepers at home, good, obedient to their own husbands, that the word of God be not blasphemed.

This scripture talks about the older women teaching the younger women and children. It says nothing about them teaching men. Why would that be?

I Corinthians 11:1-16

Time for another sermonette. □

Head Covering

The first time I read I Corinthians 11:1-16, with understanding, I said, "I must be reading this wrong. I'm missing something." It seemed to be saying women are to have their heads covered when praying and/or prophesying. Yet, I didn't know any women that did that. I knew a lot of spiritually strong women, many, much stronger in the faith than I. Could they all be wrong?

I read it again, still I felt God telling me to cover my head. Then I read, "The man is the woman's covering." I decided, that was why, my husband wasn't saved; therefore, I needed another covering. (I was just looking for that verse, it's not in I Corinthians. It may not even be in the Bible. I don't know where I got it from; it may have been satan trying to lead me astray, make me miss the real reason.)

Anyway, I was convinced and started wearing a hat to church. I did so for a year, maybe two. Then we moved and for a few weeks, I forgot my hat. When I realized I'd forgotten it I said, 'I haven't worn one all month, I can't start now.'

To justify my actions, I decided I must have forgotten because God was saying it was no longer necessary. To prove this, I took out my Bible to read the passage again. I found these words, "If a woman have long hair it is a glory to her; for her hair is given her for a covering." (V. 15) That's it! I had long hair; I was covered! (But I had long hair the first time I read this too, besides, my husband was still unsaved.)

A little later, our Pastor, who was also the adult Sunday school teacher, started a study on I Corinthians. Earlier I had asked him about the head covering and he had sidestepped the issue. So, the week he did chapter 10, I went home saying, "Finally, next week I'll find out what he thinks about this." The next week he skipped 11 and went to chapter 12.

That week I prayed, "Lord, why won't he tell us what he thinks about this. I really need an answer." The next week he came in and said he was convicted and had to back up to chapter 11. Needless to say, he believed the head covering was for today, and for all women, but he would not insist that we wear it in his church. Also, needless to say, I started wearing my hat again. One of only a few that did.

We moved again and again; I was the only woman to wear a hat to church. Again, I questioned, "Am I really, right? There are so many women; much more spiritual than I, that don't see this. I must be wrong." Then I noticed verse 16, "But if any man seem to be contentious, we have no such custom, neither do the churches of God."

I just about threw up my arms in despair. "IF YOU HAVE NO SUCH CUSTOMS, WHY DID YOU JUST SPEND THE LAST FIFTEEN VERSES TELLING US WHY WE SHOULD?" I was more confused than ever.

Then I got the Bible in 26 translations. You guessed it! The first thing I did was to go to I Corinthians 11. One translation said, "We have no such custom (of women going bear headed.) ..." (NOR) Of course! That made perfect sense. The custom of the day and church was for women to cover their heads. I had misunderstood what he was saying.

Now I was really able and ready to study this scripture and settle this issue once and for all. This is what I discovered:

I Corinthians 11:1-16

1. Be ye followers of me, even as I also am of Christ.

2. Now I praise you, brethren, that ye remember me in all things, and keep the ordinances, as I delivered them to you.

3. But I would have you know, that the head of every man is Christ; and the head of the woman is the man; and the head of Christ is God.

- We are to follow Paul as he follows Christ.

- We are to keep the ordinances that came from God, Jesus, through Paul to us.
- The head of man is Christ
- The head of woman is man
- The head of Christ is God

4. Every man praying or prophesying, having his head covered, dishonoureth his head.

5. But every woman that prayeth or prophesieth with her head uncovered dishonoureth her head: for that is even all one as if she were shaven.

6. For if the woman be not covered, let her also be shorn: but if it be a shame for a woman to be shorn or shaven, let her be covered.

- It is wrong for a man to cover his head while praying or prophesying. It is dishonoring to Christ (His head)
- It is wrong for a woman NOT to. That would be dishonoring her head – man (her husband) and be like she were shaven.
- If a woman doesn't cover her head, she should shave off all her hair. (I'm not sure, but I think it actually means cut or shaven i/e cut short.)
- If she finds that too shameful, she should cover her head. (Woman of that day caught in prostitution had their hair shaved off. They were also the only women

of that day that went out without their head covered. Perhaps, this is why they were told to shave their hair off if they refused to cover their heads. Paul could have been saying, "If you're going to act like a prostitute, take the punishment of one.)

7. For a man indeed ought not to cover his head, forasmuch as he is the image and glory of God: but the woman is the glory of the man.

8. For the man is not of the woman; but the woman of the man.

9. Neither was the man created for the woman; but the woman for the man.

10. For this cause ought the woman to have power on her head because of the angels.

- Man represents God
- Man is the glory of God
- Woman is the glory of man
- Woman was created for man
- For this reason, a woman should have the sign of authority, (The head covering), on her head; to show she is in submission to God and to her husband or father, because of the angels.
- It is believed by some that the angels watch us with amazement. God has given us free will, what are we

doing with it? They know God has told us to cover our heads, yet we don't do so and say we are submissive to Him and follow His commands. This is confusing to them.

11. Nevertheless neither is the man without the woman, neither the woman without the man, in the Lord.

12. For as the woman is of the man, even so is the man also by the woman; but all things of God.

- In God woman and man are equal

- BUT, in marriage and in the church, there is a chain of command, a right order that must be followed. Woman is last in this chain- God, Man, Woman.

13. Judge in yourselves: is it comely that a woman pray unto God uncovered?

14. Doth not even nature itself teach you, that, if a man have long hair, it is a shame unto him?

15. But if a woman have long hair, it is a glory to her: for her hair is given her for a covering.

- Men traditionally have shorter hair than women. (When you see a man with long hair, he looks like a woman and a woman with short hair, looks like a man.)

- Women were given long hair for a covering. (Does that mean that if you have long hair, you already have a covering and don't need another? NO, because verse 6 says if you don't cover your head, shave off your hair. If you do that, you will no longer have long hair.)

16. But if any man seem to be contentious, we have no such custom, neither the churches of God.

- The custom of the day was for women to cover their heads. Those who didn't were the ladies who stood on the corner trying to entice other women's husbands.

Why were these sixteen verses included here? Because Corinth was a wicked city. The women in town were starting to uncover their heads, and the women of the church were beginning to question, "Can we do that?"

They may have even tested it out, by coming to church with their head uncovered. Paul addressed this problem with a resounding, "NO! This is not right! It is not acceptable! You don't follow the customs of the world; you follow the customs of the church."

Many have read these Scriptures and said, "That is a tradition, not a commandment. We are to follow commandments, not tradition." I've also heard that one test to determine if something is tradition or command is, "Does it go back to the garden?" Here, in verses 8-10 it does, "Man was not made for woman, but woman for man, and for this cause ..."

After settling this, I said, "Okay Lord, I'm fully convinced, I will never question this again. If you want me to cover my head, I will, BUT you will have to pass it by my husband.

You see, I was no longer seeing this as a hat. When I read the word "Head covering", it seemed to be more than a hat, so I checked into it a little deeper. The Strong's concordance says this about covering: #4018 – *"Peribolaion" something thrown around one, i/e mantle, veil: covering, vesture.*

I knew my husband would think it was ugly and not want me to wear it. I was also thinking, "When praying; pray without ceasing. I should wear it all the time."

So, I prayed, "Lord if this is what you want, pass it by my husband." Then I took the scripture to him and asked what he thought of it. (Bear in mind, my husband was not saved.) He read it and said, "I don't want you to cut your hair, so cover your head when you go to church."

I explained that the scripture said when praying and that we are to pray without ceasing. He said, "You don't really do that." So, I explained what it means to pray without ceasing. And he said to wear it when I was really praying, but not when I was walking around doing other things.

That's it. I had my answer and I knew it was really what God wanted for me at that time in my life. Everything was fine, for a month or two, until I read this booklet on the head covering. In it, the author said that the covering was a privilege and an honor, and no one had the right to take that away from a woman; not even her husband.

The more I read, the more sure I was, that I should wear the covering ALL the time. When I finished the book, I got up, got my covering and put it on. I didn't care what my husband thought. I was determined that no one, not even my husband, was going to rob me of my blessing.

Before I could get out of my bedroom, I heard a voice say, "Pray." I did, and God revealed to me that I was in REBELLION. The head covering is a sign of submission, and I was not being submissive. I was making a mockery of the covering.

If I didn't wear it in submission, I shouldn't wear it at all. Yes, it is a beautiful, wonderful, sacred thing, WHEN it is worn correctly. Worn incorrectly, it means nothing and would be blaspheming the word of God. As Titus 2:5 says we are to be obedient to our own husband so not to blaspheme the word of God.

I no longer believe it is necessary to wear the covering all the time. I Corinthians 11 says, "...When praying and prophesying..." As my husband said, we don't literally pray all the time. We should be in constant commune with the Lord, and I could be wrong, but I think this is talking about a deeper, more focused prayer. Ask your husband what it means to him, and follow his conventions. His authority is law for your home.

A friend once said to me, "You must think I'm not very spiritual. I was shocked. I viewed her as being one of the most spiritual women I knew. So, I asked why she thought that. She said, "Because I don't cover my head."

I told her that if God wanted her to cover her head He would tell her so. It wasn't for me to judge her on that. I also believed that if/when He does, she may fight it a while, but she will listen, because I know she truly loves the Lord.

There have been many times when I felt I needed the covering, but didn't have it on. At those times, God literally covered me. I felt the covering on my head more completely and securely at that moment then at the times I did have it on. If you submit to God, and to your husband, God will see you through anything.

So, yes, I totally believe the head covering is for today and for all women, BUT, if your husband says no, pray and wait until God changes his heart and he says yes. (END)

Ephesians 5:22-24

Wives, submit yourselves unto your own husbands, as unto the Lord. For the husband is the head of the wife, even as Christ is the head of the church: and he is the saviour of the body. Therefore as the church is subject unto Christ, so let the wives be to their own husbands in every thing.

Notice this says "Your OWN husband". First it tells you to submit, then it tells you why; because the husband is head of the wife, AS Christ is head of the church. It's not about men being better than women, it is about position (Chain of command).

I Peter 3:1-2

Likewise, ye wives, be in subjection to your own husbands; that, if any obey not the word, they also may without the word be won by the conversation of the wives; While they behold your chaste conversation coupled with fear.

Conversation here means behavior, it's what you do, not what you say. And fear means respect, you should not be afraid of your husband. Respect comes from love and admiration, not from being afraid.

Notice it says here that you are to submit to your OWN husband, EVEN IF he does NOT believe. So, are you really submissive to God and following what He commands, if you are not submissive to your husband? I think not!

You may think these verses are very much against women; you may even call them chauvinistic. But, in truth, they are not. Man was formed first and is our earthly example of God. Woman came from man and represents the church.

The church is NEVER greater than, nor even equal to God. Therefore, woman cannot be equal to man in the chain of command. Women are equal to men in Christ there is no difference. But, in the church and home we MUST keep divine order.

So, what is the woman's place in the church and home? Right beside her husband, following his lead and supporting his endeavors. Does this mean that she cannot have her own ministry in the church? No, but her ministry should be complimenting his and meet his approval.

The one exception is when he is not saved and not in church. Even then, if he does not want you to take on the added responsibility of this ministry, you do not do it. He is still the head of your home and you are still to be submissive to him. With the one exception of abuse, we talked of earlier.

In the home, a woman is to fulfill Titus 2:4-5, remembering that her husband's word is law for her home. If she does not agree with him, she may go to him privately and appeal his decision. She is there as a helper to him and sometimes has better insight in certain matters. BUT, after she has said her piece, she must accept his final answer on the matter.

In the church, she may be a teacher of women and children, but NEVER, NEVER of men. If the men of the church are teaching things that she believes to be wrong, she should go to her husband. Let him approach the men in question, or the pastor, if he agrees that it is wrong. If her husband doesn't go to church, then she should go to the man doing the teaching, then pastor, seeking understanding not accusingly. If the teaching continues, and after prayer, she still feels it is wrong, perhaps it is time to find a new church.

If you're thinking the church will fall because the men won't do anything if the women stop leading everything, don't worry about it. That is not your concern. You need to do what God has called you to do. No more and no less.

If the men don't take their rightful place, then God will deal with them. But if you step out of your rightful place to take over theirs; then God has to deal with you. Two wrongs do not make a right. If the women know their place and stay in it, praying that God will raise up the men he wants in leadership, He will do so. If the church falls, maybe it wasn't meant to be there in the first place. Don't try to tell God how to do things. He knows what is best.

Moving on, we find the virtuous wife plants a vineyard. What is a vineyard, if not a place for growing grapes? In the dictionary, definition number two tells us: *area of action or field of endeavor, esp. one of a spiritual nature.*

I've always wanted to have grapes growing through the slats of my porch roof. Right now, I don't have one, but some day... That would take care of definition number one, but what about the more important definition number two? For me, it is to have an open home, where we can minister as a family to other families. What and where is your vineyard?

"She girds her loins with strength." What does gird mean?

- *To surround or encircle with a belt or girdle. To prepare oneself for action. To invest, clothe, equip, endue.*

Loins:

- *Strongs 4975 From an unused root mean- to be slender; Prep. The waist or small of the back. Only in plur. The loins- + grayhound, loins, side.*
    - This again lends to the idea of staying in shape, of not having a lot of excess weight. A good diet and exercise program might be in order ☺

Have you invested the time to surround yourself with strength, so that you are prepared for action? Remember, the strength of God's word is more powerful than physical strength. We face challenges every day that would send many men to their knees. Yet, God has given us all we need to meet them head on and win. It is our "Flax" qualities showing through. That "Strength in a pretty package" is indeed the perfect example of a woman's strength.

Notice, she gives special attention to strengthening her arms. Could it be that she will need strong arms for most of her work? I'm sure she's not strengthening them for vanity purposes, nor for protection. She has her husband for that. She doesn't sound like a paper pusher either. No, she was a worker, and a caregiver.

Being her lamp does not go out at night and that fact is mentioned in connection with her merchandise being good, it is safe to assume that she works at night on something worthwhile to supplement the family income.

Therefore, we can also assume that her business was a home business, since she wouldn't be burning the midnight oil outside. In those days, no good person worked outside the home at night. When the sun went down, good and honest men and women stayed in. They went to bed to get the rest they needed for the full day ahead.

An interesting note here is how she uses her time. The order in which she does things each day shows us where we should be placing our priorities.

1. She rises early, probably the first one up by a good hour, to prepare meals for her family and get ready for the day's tasks.

2. She takes care of the needs of her household; sees that everyone has everything they need. They know they are loved by the special care she gives each one.

3. She sees to it that the house is clean and in order.

4. She has a ministry, helping the poor. Perhaps giving them food or clothing; or better yet, a job, or teaching them skills for a job.

5. Her HOME business. (Although 2-4 are not spelled out for us, we know they are there from verses 19-22 & 27.) We know the business comes last because:

    a. She would not be helping the poor or needy at night when most would be in bed and no virtuous woman would be out.

    b. That is the only time this passage mentions her lamp being on.

Now, to clear up the question of why I think today's virtuous wife would have a home-based business and not work outside the home:

1. The list above shows us how important her family is to her. She would not trust their care to someone who did not love them as she does.

2. Titus 2:5, as mentioned earlier, states that women are to be "keepers at home". (Remember keepers comes from the Greek word meaning stay-er) How can you be a keeper (stayer) at home while working outside the home? Notice it doesn't say "housekeeper" as some interpret it, meaning one who cleans house. This is not just about keeping a clean house, which does not require all day every day.

3. "Keeper" means*: (Keep) to retain in one's possession, power or control. To cause to continue in some specified place, condition, relation, or position. To continue, maintain or preserve. To be faithful to, abide by. To look after the affairs of. To provide the necessities of life for, support. To keep from harm, guard, defend. To take care of, watch over, tend.*

    a. How can you do all that when your family is at home and you're not? Even though I know you're not and shouldn't be with them 24 hours a day, you should be easily accessible. You're not always when working outside the home. *To remain in, at, or on.* (in other words; "Stay-at-home wife and mother")

    b. *(Keeper) Person who protects, tends, or is responsible for someone or something.* (It is our job to protect, tend to and be responsible for the home and everything connected to it. That does not mean we are to take over leadership in the home. These are two different positions. The keeper is under the authority of the Leader.)

4. Stayer: Somebody or something that stays. Somebody with much stamina and persistence.

This should be obvious, but I just want to confirm I'm not saying you need to stay home 24/7. There are things that need to be done outside the home environment. But her main focus is understood to be at home.

This is a big topic and highly debated. To cover it fully would require a book. In fact, there were four excellent books written on this subject. Probably more, but these are the ones I've read:

a. "A Full Quiver" by Rick and Jan Hess

b. "Free to Stay Home" by Mrilee Horton

c. "The Way Home" by Mary Pride

d. "All The Way Home" by Mary Pride

Another thing that impressed me with this lady is that she gets up real early, stays up real late, keeps busy all day and NEVER complains. She is not selfish, but does all she can for others, expecting nothing in return. Yes, she does care for herself too, but not first.

Least we get things out of perspective here; we need to remember the words of Solomon in:

Psalms 127:1-2

Except the Lord build the house, they labour in vain that build it: except the Lord keep the city, the watchman waketh but in vain. It is vain for you to rise up early, to sit up late, to eat the bread of sorrows: for so he giveth his beloved sleep.

Remember, it is believed to be Solomon's mother who inspired this writing on the virtuous wife. There is a balance; neither he nor she was saying to go all day and night without sleep. A virtuous wife needs her sleep.

We must "always remember and never forget" that, whatever we do and where ever we do it, we should always do the best we can do. Don't settle for second best, remember, she perceived that her merchandise was good.

Here we go again! That distaff, that she stretches her hand out to, brings us home once more. Do you know what it is? In case you don't, I'll quote Webster's one more time.

Distaff:

1. Stick used for spinning, usually cleft at one end, on which wool, flax, cotton, or other fibers are held and from which they are drawn off and twisted into thread by hand onto a spindle.

2. Woman's work, concerns or domain.

I'm sure the women's lib movement hates this word. They would like us to believe there is no such thing as "Women's work", but that men and women are equal and do all work equally. (Unless they can talk the men into staying home and taking care of the home full time.)

God gave us a special job to do that comes with very special concerns and needs special care. He gave US domain over this area. Why? Because, He gave US the special ability to be able to handle it. It is up to us, if we don't no one else will.

Many men are trying to be House husbands today, but they don't have the God given abilities to carry out all that the job requires. No home will be run as it should be, if we are not following God's order.

Notice the first definition. What is that stick doing? It is holding the wool, flax, cotton & other fibers, (Remember how these relate to women.) and twists them together to make one strong, pretty thread. (As you know, the Bible tells us, a three-strand thread is not quickly broken.)

Need I say what I'm thinking, or have you already figured it out? Perhaps being a keeper/stayer at home is what keeps us the way God intended us to be. Those pretty fibers woven together into a pretty strong thread, that's our life.

We have a big responsibility here. Are we going to let someone else tell us our life is worthless if we don't go out and get a job? Are we going to listen to others telling us that our family will never survive if we don't bring home our share of the bacon? Will we have a family to survive if we cave in to other's concerns and demands?

Have you thought about when the family started decaying? It was the same time women took off their head coverings, cut their hair, put on pants and went to work outside the home.

Yes, I know there are many women who have gone out into the working world and manage family and career. But, what have they given up to do that? Yes, some still have their families with them. Some have beautiful Christian children, but many more are having multiple hidden problems with those same beautiful Christian children.

If you are a working mom right now, please take this challenge. Talk to your children. Ask them for a truthful answer to this question. Tell them you really want to know what they think, not what they think you want to hear. Ask them if they would rather have you home with them or those big expensive toys you were only able to get because mom was working.

If they say: "You"; what they're really saying is, "Mom, you're not there when I need you." If they say "The toys"; They're saying, "Mom, I don't feel you really care about me, so I'll take what I can get. Besides, all my friends' moms work and if I'm going to fit in, I have to keep up with the latest trinkets. What they hope you don't realize is, "if you're home, it won't be as easy to sneak out and do all those things you don't want me to do." Sorry, I didn't intend this to be a trick question. I don't always think ahead when I write.

What do you really want, a family that loves each other, or a group of people living under the same roof worshiping money? The best excuse of all is "We need the second income to pay the mortgage. We're not buying anything we don't need." There's an old saying "Let go and let God." Many have tried it. I've heard many success stories that go something like this:

"We were $X,000 in debt, not able to pay the bills with two incomes. Then God told us that my wife was to stop working. I said, but Lord, we can't make it now, how can we make it with our income cut in half? He said just do it; so, we did. That week God worked a miracle."

From there the story has several endings,

- "I put my check in the bank, pay our tithe, then our bills, and there's money left over."
- "We got an anonymous check in the mail."
- "I received a promotion that gave us more money than when my wife was working."
- "We found many ways to save money by doing things different, or even doing without things we thought we needed, but found we didn't."
- "We were able to start a home-based business that brought in more money than my wife's job did."

So, let go and let God. What more can I say?

I do want to say this, when I first started this book, I wanted to show that whether you worked in or outside the home, was between you and God. But, as I got deeper and deeper into this, I realized this passage is about a woman who stays home to raise and care for her family.

Even though her children are not boldly mentioned, it is understood she does have them. They do not prevent her from doing all these other things, nor does she leave their care to someone else.

When I was first married I worked outside the home until my first child, then I stayed home with them, although my husband was not in total agreement, he kind of understood it would be more expensive to get a full-time baby sitter.

When I remarried, although we had no children at home, my husband believed as I did that, my place was in the home; it was his job to provide for the family.

He made a little over $1400 a month. Our bills totaled a little over $1400 not including food, gas and the tithe. But we still, paid the tithe, the bills, kept food in the house and the truck on the road.

Yes, money was tight, but God saw us through. AND, things were a thousand times better than they were with my first husband, even though he made five times as much.

But, about a year later my husband decided I did need to go to work outside the home. After doing so he started drinking again and pulled away from Church. We got deeper and deeper in debt. He hurt his back one last time, this time it never fully recovered and he is out of work on permanent disability.

But the story does not end there. Because of the settlement we were able to get our dream home setting on 58 acres. We were planning on selling our first home and using that to pay off the excess bills, but that didn't happen, so, we were again swamped with bills.

BUT he went back to church, the Lord took away all desire for booze and our spiritual life went to an all-time high.

I was still working outside the home trying to find a way to pay off enough bills so I could stay home. I wanted to take the above advice, but he wasn't yet ready to do so. I kept working.

That was when I developed little bumps on the back of my head. Never could discover what they were, nothing I did would get rid of them.

Sometimes they would disappear for a day but come right back. I felt it was spiritual. It had to do with me working outside the home where I didn't belong. I was taking over the headship in in this area. My husband didn't see this but those bumps remained on my head for 5-7 years, until the day I gave my 2-week notice. That day they disappeared and have not returned.

I have been working at home for 4 years. I make twice the money I did when I worked outside the home, and our bills are decreasing not increasing for the first time since we've been married.

Other translations say:

> "She perceiveth that her traffic is successful" (SPRL)

What exactly does that mean? She has a clear path so people can move through her house easily and quickly?

> "She perceives that her grains are good:" (ABPS)

Okay, at least grains are a type of merchandise, but they are not the only type. While it did say earlier that she planted a field, there are many things other than grain that could have been planted. Also, you usually note that your crops are good while they are still in the field during daylight hours. (Okay, that's probably not what they meant here.)

> "She sees that her marketing is of profit to her." (BAS)

> "She sees that her business goes well." (NEB)

I guess?

> "She puts her hands to the cloth-working rod, and her fingers take the wheel."

When I first read that I thought "A woman libber must have written that one. Couldn't bring herself to using the word "distaff". "Yes, this does basically describe what a distaff and spindle do, in relation to the spinning wheel. But what about the second meaning for the word Distaff? It's not there at all. Then there's the alternate meaning for "Spindle" *To shoot or grow in a long slender stalk or body.* (Could that be talking about raising your children? Or perhaps taking care of your own body?)

Discussion 6

She stretcheth out her hand to the poor; yea, she reacheth forth her hands to the needy. Pro. 31: 20

1. Do you stretch out your hand to the poor and needy? Who are the needy?

2. In what ways, in and out of the home, can we help?

3. What should your attitude be while serving in these ways?

4. Why should we reach out?

CH 6

She stretcheth out her hand to the poor; yea, she reacheth forth her hands to the needy. Pro. 31: 20

While I believe this lady did her ministry work before her job, or at least placed more value on the ministry than on the job, I believe it is mentioned after because she did not do it every day. This type of ministry is one that comes up here and there. When it is needed, you do it, but you don't see the need every day.

Those that God can depend on He uses. If you want to be used by God, you have to be available. He will put a man on the sidewalk outside your house that needs that pair of shoes in your closet no one can wear, but if you're at work, you'll miss him.

God will tell you who needs a special call, but if you are in the middle of a big important meeting, she won't be there when you get to her. God has used many women throughout history. In the days when education and the world of religion belonged to men, He used women. Why? They were available.

Remember Debra, she sat under a tree in her yard and many people came to her for direction and to settle disputes. Her name comes up often as proof that women can minister in the church to men. But nowhere have I read that she did that. Yes, men came to her with questions and for settlement of disputes, and yes she was a judge; but she did not minister in the church, or go to them, they came to her. She was a judge that worked at home.

Okay, so that's MY interpretation. I don't really know where Debra's tree was and many would disagree with me about it being in her own back yard, or front yard for that matter. But does anybody really know? In the light of this teaching, don't you think it's possible that I might be right?

Interesting sidebar. Remember Rebeca's nurse, Deborah? When she died they buried her under an oak that they called Allon-bachuth which means Oak of Weeping. Some believe this is the same Oak that years later Judge Deborah sat under to judge the people.

By the way, I don't think women were as dumb and uneducated as they would have us believe today. They didn't have schools, so where did the boys learn to read and write? From their moms; yes, women taught the children. Yes, there were many untaught men in those days, but I wonder if that didn't simply mean they didn't know five or six languages. It was normal in those days for a man to speak several languages.

Now I know, someone is going to say they did have schools. Yes, the higher educated men did get an education somewhere other than home. I believe mostly at the synagogue, but I could be wrong. But still, your basic early learning was done at home.

Yes, you are right, I am harping on this. And yes, many women have been used mightily in the work place. But, then too, unsaved men have preached sermons that lead many to the Lord. Sometimes, being in the wrong place at the right time can benefit someone else. But more good could be done if you were in the right place.

I don't want to offend you if you happen to be one of those women in the workplace, or a pastor of a church, and I don't want to tell you what to do. I believe God will talk to all Christians. Since you are accountable to Him for what He tells you to do, you are the one responsible to find out what He is telling you.

I also believe, especially today, when we've gotten so far away from God's original plans, that He calls different people into different things. I used to believe that some women did belong in the work place, now I'm not so sure. Are you?

If you come up to me, and say, "God told me to keep my job." I'm not going to tell you you're wrong, nor start insisting that you're not living a good Christian life, because you don't happen to agree with me. I do hope though, that you are not guilty of insisting God is telling you to keep working, because you can't see any other way to make ends meet, or because you don't think you could stand to be home with the children all day.

PRAY ABOUT IT AND BE SURE!

Another problem you may have is that your husband is insisting that you work. If this is truly the case and it's not you wanting to work and him allowing it, pray that God will open your husband's eyes to the truth of His Word. Then go to your husband with the scriptures (and perhaps even the discussion in chapter 5 of this book).

Ask him to study them and tell you what he thinks. Whether he is a Christian or not, God can change his mind. Your place is to go with his decision on the matter. If he decides that you should work outside the home, do so, but keep praying for God's will in this matter.

I'm about to quote another old saying. One I've always hated because too many people use it as an excuse not to give, not to reach out to the needy. But I'm adding my own ending to bring things back into prospective:

Charity begins at home. BUT IT DOESN'T END THERE!

Yes, I do agree, charity does indeed begin at home. We must teach our children to give, by giving to them. We must teach them how to love, by loving them. But if we never give to and love those outside our household, our children will never learn the great Biblical truth; "It is more blessed to give then to receive." (Acts 20:35) We will rob them of that wonderful opportunity and blessing.

To get a better understanding of some ways we can extend our hand to the poor and needy, let's consult God's word:

Matthew 25:33-40

For I was an hungred, and ye gave me meat: I was thirsty, and ye gave me drink: I was a stranger, and ye took me in: Naked, and ye clothed me: I was sick, and ye visited me: I was in prison, and ye came unto me. Then shall the righteous answer him, saying, Lord, when saw we thee an hungred, and fed thee? or thirsty, and gave thee drink? When saw we thee a stranger, and took thee in? or naked, and clothed thee? Or when saw we thee sick, or in prison, and came unto thee? And the King shall answer and say unto them, Verily I say unto you, Inasmuch as ye have done it unto one of the least of these my brethren, ye have done it unto me.

We are all God's children; yes, some of us are stubborn, uncaring, unyielding, set in our ways; but we are still His children. He loves us, sometimes He has to use a stronger hand to teach us to love and show compassion. That is why he says, 'what you do to the least of these, you do to Me.' We are a part of Him; and He is a part of them.

Luke 6:30-38

Give to every man that asketh of thee; and of him that taketh away thy goods ask them not again. And as ye would that men should do to you, do ye also to them

likewise. For if ye love them which love you, what thank have ye? for sinners also love those that love them. And if ye do good to them which do good to you, what thank have ye? for sinners also do even the same. And if ye lend to them of whom ye hope to receive, what thank have ye? for sinners also lend to sinners, to receive as much again. But love ye your enemies, and do good, and lend, hoping for nothing again; and your reward shall be great, and ye shall be the children of the Highest: for he is kind unto the unthankful and to the evil. Be ye therefore merciful, as your Father also is merciful. Judge not, and ye shall not be judged: condemn not, and ye shall not be condemned: forgive, and ye shall be forgiven: Give, and it shall be given unto you; good measure, pressed down, and shaken together, and running over, shall men give into your bosom. For with the same measure that ye mete withal it shall be measured to you again.

God gave everything for us, yet He has so much more He wants to give us. Can't we give a little?

Exodus 23:11

But the seventh year thou shalt let it (the land) **rest and lie still; that the poor of thy people may eat: and what they leave the beasts of the field shall eat. In like manner thou shalt deal with thy vineyard, and with thy oliveyard**.

This passage comes under the law of sabbaths. There is much debate as to whether we should be following these laws today. The whole legalism/Grace thing is very complicated and I'm not here to debate that, but in the relationship of charity, it gives us something to think about. As we are to rest from our work, on the seventh day of each week, we are to allow our gardens to rest in the seventh year. Whatever grows of its own should be left for the poor.

The other six years when you harvest you are to leave the corners, not harvest everything, but again, to leave some for the poor. Therefore, if a bum comes to your door, don't turn him away, invite him to pick from your garden for his family. Our gardens should be open to the gleaners, not just in the seventh year, but every year.

Yes, there were set rules to be followed and you need to decide what they are for your home and garden. For more information on this, you could read the book of Ruth. The books of law also have a lot to say on this matter. Do a word study on "gleaning". I find this topic very interesting and inspiring.

Leviticus 19:10

And thou shalt not glean thy vineyard, neither shalt thou gather every grape of thy vineyard; thou shalt leave them for the poor and stranger: I am the Lord your God. (See also Lev. 23:22)

Don't gate up your gardens, allow others in. Show them love and respect.

Leviticus 25:35-37

And if a man purchase of the Levites, then the house that was sold, and the city of his possession, shall go out in the year of jubile: for the houses of the cities of the Levites are their possession among the children of

Israel. But the field of the suburbs of their cities may not be sold; for it is their perpetual possession. And if thy brother be waxen poor, and fallen in decay with thee; then thou shalt relieve him: yea, though he be a stranger, or a sojourner; that he may live with thee. Take thou no usury of him, or increase: but fear thy God; that thy brother may live with thee. Thou shalt not give him thy money upon usury, nor lend him thy victuals for increase.

Open your heart and your home. YES, to the poor, those with nothing; yes, even to strangers. You say this was written in a different time. Yes, it was, but there were robbers and murders then too. Yet, God gave this command.

Ecclesiastes tells us there is nothing new under the sun. Heb 13:8 tells us that Jesus is the same yesterday, today and forever. His Word does not change. His hand is not shortened, that He cannot save. (Is. 59:1)

Deuteronomy 15:11

For the poor shall never cease out of the land: therefore I command thee, saying, Thou shalt open thine hand wide unto thy brother, to thy poor, and to thy needy, in thy land.

The poor will always be with us; it is our duty to help them.

Proverbs 14:20-21

The poor is hated even of his own neighbour: but the rich hath many friends. He that despiseth his neighbour sinneth: but he that hath mercy on the poor, happy is he.

Are we sinning in this matter? Yes, we are. Many of us look down on the poor. This should not be; we need to treat them with respect. Show them mercy as our Heavenly Father showed us mercy.

Proverbs 14:31

He that oppresseth the poor reproacheth his Maker: but he that honoureth him hath mercy on the poor.

When we do not treat the poor appropriately, we dishonor God; we sadden His heart. But we show Him honor when we have mercy on the poor and treat them with respect.

Proverbs 28:27

He that giveth unto the poor shall not lack: but he that hideth his eyes shall have many a curse.

You want to be rich? Give! It sounds like a contradiction; how can you get rich if you are always giving away what you have? But that is one of God's laws: **Luke 6:38 Give, and it shall be given unto you; good measure, pressed down, and shaken together, and running over, shall men give into your bosom. For with the same measure that ye mete withal it shall be measured to you again. KJV** So remember, give and it will come back to you, hold on with a tight hand and it will slip through your fingers.

Proverbs 31:8-9

Open thy mouth for the dumb in the cause of all such as are appointed to destruction. Open thy mouth, judge righteously, and plead the cause of the poor and needy.

Speak for those who cannot speak. Speak the truth. Judge by the facts not the social class.

Matthew 19:21

Jesus said unto him, If thou wilt be perfect, go and sell that thou hast, and give to the poor, and thou shalt have treasure in heaven: and come and follow me.

You want to obtain perfection? It is possible. Sell all that you have and give the proceeds to those in need. Then follow Jesus. Ask what would Jesus do and do it.

Luke 14:13-14

But when thou makest a feast, call the poor, the maimed, the lame, the blind: And thou shalt be blessed; for they cannot recompense thee: for thou shalt be recompensed at the resurrection of the just.

Make a feast for those who cannot pay you back; for those who truly need it, and expect nothing in return. God will repay you when the time is right, in the way you need.

I Corinthians 13:3

And though I bestow all my goods to feed the poor, and though I give my body to be burned, and have not charity, it profiteth me nothing.

Giving alone is not enough. If you give with a begrudging heart no one benefits. It will not be a blessing to the one receiving because they will know you really didn't want to give it and won't be able to enjoy it. It won't be a blessing to you, because God says to give willingly, with a cheerful heart. You must love, give of yourself; the one thing no one else can give. Giving with a grateful heart brings love and peace.

While we put verses like these into practice, we must not forget the ones that balance them. If we do, we may end up doing more harm than good. Our brother needs to know we care and are there for him, but not to the point of making him lazy and unable to care for himself. So, remember:

II Thessalonians 3:10-13

For even when we were with you, this we commanded you, that if any would not work, neither should he eat. For we hear that there are some which walk among you disorderly, working not at all, but are busybodies. Now them that are such we command and exhort by our Lord Jesus Christ, that with quietness they work, and eat their own bread. But ye, brethren, be not weary in well doing.

If you are lazy you have not earned the blessing of food. 'Idol hands are the devil's playground.' Busybodies have no place in God's kingdom. We are not to enable the lazy. They need to get out and work. They need to earn a living, buy their own bread, but we are to help those who can't.

This scripture is talking about able bodied people who refused to work. Not those who were sick or unable to work.

Before we leave this topic take a look at this:

Ezekiel 16:49

Behold, this was the iniquity of thy sister Sodom, pride, fulness of bread, and abundance of idleness was

in her and in her daughters, neither did she strengthen the hand of the poor and needy.

We all know the fate of Sodom and Gomorra and we all know what caused it. But, had any of us, until now, noticed that listed with their sins was the great sin of not reaching out to the poor and needy?

God thought it worthy of being mentioned. He places great value on this act of mercy. Let us not be found guilty of not sharing what we have, however much or little it is. Do not become sounding brass or a tinkling cymbal.

Also, notice listed here, is "abundance of idleness."

I Corinthians 13:1

Though I speak with the tongues of men and of angels, and have not charity, I am become as sounding brass, or a tinkling cymbal.

Charity here is love. What greater love can you have than to help a brother or stranger in need?

Other translations say:

> "Kindly is her welcome to the poor, her purse ever open to those in need." (KNOX)
>
> > Of course, you caught the problems here. Right? You can welcome the poor without helping them; and if you always have your purse open, you may be stopping God from reaching them, or stopping them from helping themselves.

Discussion 7

She is not afraid of the snow for her household: for all her household are clothed with scarlet. She maketh herself coverings of tapestry; her clothing is silk and purple. Her husband is known in the gates, when he sitteth among the elders of the land. She maketh fine linen, and selleth it; and delivereth girdles unto the merchant. Strength and honour are her clothing; and she shall rejoice in time to come. Pro. 31:21-25

1. What is the significance of: a) Scarlet b) rich c) tapestry d) linen e) silk f) purple?
2. How should we apply these Qualities to ourselves, our marriage, our family?
3. Why spend all that money on tapestry and linen? Wouldn't that money be better spent somewhere else?
4. Is your husband known in town? What can you do to enhance his standing with the elders?
5. If we want to help add to the family income, do we have to make things to sell, or can we do something else?
6. A woman who does all this doesn't have time to rejoice. She'd be way too tired, so how can we rejoice in times to come?

CH 7

She is not afraid of the snow for her household: for all her household are clothed with scarlet. She maketh herself coverings of tapestry; her clothing is silk and purple. Her husband is known in the gates, when he sitteth among the elders of the land. She maketh fine linen, and selleth it; and delivereth girdles unto the merchant. Strength and honour are her clothing; and she shall rejoice in time to come. Pro. 31:21-25

Let's look for a minute at a couple of definitions for snow. First:

Small white spots on a television screen as a result of WEAK RECEPTION.

I realize I'm taking this slightly out of context, but when I read that, it hit me, "This lady does not have to fear her family getting weak reception." And why not? Because, she's there for them, they have good communication. They know she loves them. If she never once told them, they would still know. Yet, I have a feeling, not a day passed without the words, "I love you" being spoken. (With that thought in mind, I'm not so sure I took it out of context.)

The second is the slang: (Snow Job)

To overpower with insincere flattery, especially in order to deceive.

Again, this woman doesn't have to fear her family being taken in by someone who means them harm. Why?

1. Because she knows God will take care of them.

2. She taught them well, how to "lean not on their own understanding" but to trust God.

3. She has made her home a place of safety, where they can grow to feel good about themselves, and know how to think for themselves.

4. They are not so starved for affection, or attention, that they will believe anything anyone says, as long as they pay some attention to them.

Deception is a deadly game and one of satan's most powerful tools. We should pray every day that we are not deceived, that our family is not deceived. Pray that they know they can come to us with anything and that we will respond correctly when they do come. Don't assume they know, take an active interest in their life.

All of her household was clothed with Scarlet, a symbol of royalty. Sounds like they were abundantly loved and cared for.

This lady knows how to sew! Do you? Do you care? Should you? Like it or not, sewing is a big part of our job. Could you imagine throwing out a fifty-dollar dress? Just because the seam gave out? (Today I guess we would have to say a $500 dress.)

NO, you don't have to be an avid sewer just to put on a button or sew up a seam. But, just think of the creations you could make and the money you could save if you only really knew how to sew!

Okay, so you don't know and you really don't want to learn. Does that mean you could never be even a modern-day virtuous wife? You bet ya! Is that enough to get you to start sewing? Na, I didn't think so. All joking aside, I don't really think rather you sew or not makes that much of a difference to God.

As Marilee Horton points out in her book, "Free to Stay Home" if you watch the sales, and go to factory outlets and/or second hand stores, you can quite often buy readymade clothes cheaper than you can make them. Above sewing, God calls us to be good Stewards.

If you really want to get technical, it says she made tapestry. It doesn't say she made all her clothes. Although it says the tapestry was used as coverings for herself, so, she probably did. Most women in that time period did and by hand too. They didn't have sewing machines then. (Although, tapestry was probably done on a loom.)

Ah, but her clothing is silk and purple. What difference does fabric and color make? Not much. But... these are two of the best. Silk is a fine soft thread and makes a delicate cloth. (Made of fine workmanship, produced a beautiful garment.) Purple was very hard to come by, therefore quite expensive. She spared no expense.

I think this is talking more about who she was than about what she wore. She was a lady that spared no expense when it came to finishing her tasks and doing for others.

Strength and honor are her clothing. They would have to be, or she would never have become the virtuous woman she was. She needs strength of body to perform all her daily chores and strength of character since she would not be virtuous if she lied, stole or wasn't kind to others. She is a woman of honor. You can trust her with your life, many probably did. When you go to her with a problem, she will seek God for the answer.

Next, she makes fine linen and sells it, and girdles for the merchants. This was her home business that we talked of earlier. You can be sure; if she was selling this stuff, it was well made. I know not everyone is cut out to be a fine seamstress. Some take lessons for years and just can't get the hang of it. They weren't gifted in that area; they are gifted in another. So, find where your gifts lie and base your home business on that.

Yes, right or wrong, our husband is known at the city gate, partly by what kind of wife he has. I'm inclined to say rightly, because it goes to show what kind of judgment he has. Also, (if you're sensitive to this subject, sorry, but you need to work on it; and I need to say it) it shows how well he rules his home. If he doesn't have control at home, he probably won't be much good at business either.

How is your husband known? As having a wife who is loving and kind to all, or hateful and selfish? Wise and discerning, or wasteful and foolish? Someone who will talk about anyone at any time, or one who can be trusted to keep a confidence? One who is faithful, or one who is always looking at what or who doesn't belong to her? Someone who cares about others, or only cares about herself? Do you show off your husband well in those city gates? Or does he hang his head in shame when your name comes up?

The time has come, we should all be rejoicing! And why? Because we're almost to the end of this book! Just one more, short chapter and that is one of high praise for all the work you've done. Then, we're DONE; until the next time you read this book. And, I hope there will be a next time. It won't be so bad, I promise! You've already corrected all those things that hit you so hard this time.

But a virtuous wife will keep working. She will not slack. She will always strive to better herself, to be better than the day before.

She does not sweep the little annoyances under the rug, because she knows they will get bigger and bigger until dealt with. Then they will be harder and harder to deal with.

Other translations say:

> "With all her servants warmly clothed. She makes her own quilts," (JERUS)
>
> What about her family?
>
> "...for they are wrapped in two clocks." (NEB)
>
> Do you wear two coats in the winter? Maybe a sweater under a coat, but two coats?
>
> Rejoice in time to come:
>
> "she laugheth at the time (Days) to come" (ASV, RHM & AAT)
>
> "Laughs at the future." (ABPS)
>
> That sounds like she thinks it's a big joke. Rejoicing is much more than laughing.

Discussion 8

She openeth her mouth with wisdom; and in her tongue is the law of kindness. She looketh well to the ways of her household, and eateth not the bread of idleness. Her children arise up, and call her blessed; her husband also, and he praiseth her. Many daughters have done virtuously, but thou excellest them all. Favour is deceitful, and beauty is vain: but a woman that feareth the Lord, she shall be praised. Give her of the fruit of her hands; and let her own works praise her in the gates. Pro. 31:26-31

1. Where do you get wisdom?

2. What is the law of kindness?

3. Do we have to stay home in order to be good mothers and look after our children?

4. Let's get real! You don't have to be right there all the time to be watching over them. Right?

5. What is "Bread of Idleness"?

6. Why are charm and beauty so bad?

7. Why will a woman who fears the Lord be praised over one who does great things, but doesn't fear the Lord?

CH 8

She openeth her mouth with wisdom; and in her tongue is the law of kindness. She looketh well to the ways of her household, and eateth not the bread of idleness. Her children arise up, and call her blessed; her husband also, and he praiseth her. Many daughters have done virtuously, but thou excellest them all. Favour is deceitful, and beauty is vain: but a woman that feareth the Lord, she shall be praised. Give her of the fruit of her hands; and let her own works praise her in the gates. Pro. 31:26-31

Notice, this lady doesn't moan and complain, but rather speaks from the Word, with love. You know she reads and studies her Bible daily; otherwise, she wouldn't have the wisdom with which to speak. For God says the wisdom of the world is foolishness. Besides, where else would she have even heard of the law of kindness?

Her tongue, that very interesting topic comes up again! Every virtuous wife should be well versed in James 3. For no matter how well, you do in every other area we've talked about in this book, it won't mean too much, if you don't control your tongue. (You may want to look through your notes on Ch. 2 and do the James 3 study again.)

A virtuous mother hen is what I think of when I read, "She watches over the ways of her household." I can almost see her setting on a cloud overlooking all her children. Watching what they do all day, ready to step in on a second's notice if they need her. How much love she has for her family!

Of course, we know she doesn't set around all day just watching. That would be very "idle" of her. She doesn't have the time, nor the desire, to be idle. She wants to please God, and He hates idleness. He knows how much trouble that would create for all of us.

Do your children call you blessed? Are they glad that you are their mother? Many parents today feel their "kids" don't appreciate anything. They probably don't, but why is that? What are your actions and attitudes telling your children?

"Get away from me kid, I don't have time for you and your minor little problems! I have my own to worry about." "If we're going to have the finer things of life I have to work, after all, things are more important than you."

How could anyone love, respect, admire, or call blessed someone that, by their own actions and attitudes, are telling them that they're nothing, not worth their time? If you want to receive the praise of your husband and children, you have to earn it. You need to be there for them, no matter how small their problem is, it is big to them.

I'm sure that when your children want to fit in with the crowd by going out and drinking till all hours, they don't exactly love you when you say "no". At least they won't let you know they liked having that easy out. But any child, regardless of age, will speak well of his/her mother if:

1. He doesn't see signs of hypocrisy:

    a. Tell them not to do something then turn around and do it yourself. (Smoke, drink, swear, watch TV before getting chores done, snack before a meal, etc.)

2. Your love is in actions, not just words.

    a. "I love you, make yourself a sandwich, I'm going to my meeting" as you open the door, "How was school today?" almost before they answer, "That's nice. Don't stay up to late, gotta go, lov ya, bye." (In case you were wondering, those actions speak volumes, but they don't say I love you, like this next example does.)

    b. "Oh, good, you're home. I wanted to find out how that test went before I left. I know you were worried about it." (Listen to the whole fifteen-minute ordeal). "How about tryouts, Make the team?" "That's great! Supper's in the oven and I made brownies for your snack. Hopefully, I'll be back before you have to go to bed. Bye, Lov ya." (By the way, this scenario should be the exception not the rule. Things you have to do outside the home should be done when the rest of the family is not home, as much as possible.)

3. Spend real time with them, letting them get to know the real you and getting to know the real them.

How about your husband? Does he praise you while setting with the elders at the city gate? Does he have anything to praise you for? Perhaps the way you always drag him down by saying something negative when he comes through the door after work. Or that long "Honey do" list you give him every weekend. (You're not still doing those things are you? Of course not, cause you're a virtuous wife now.)

Maybe that neat way you have of leaving the moment he comes home for that meeting you can't miss. "Oh, Johnnie's at Jimmie's, you have to pick him up in ten minutes." Or that nice greeting of toys all over the floor, no supper to be seen and no family in sight; because you just had to run over to Joan's to see that new dress she just bought.

Now, we know you're not that bad, if you were God would not say of you, "Many have done well, but you excel them all." If you've made it this far through this book you really do excel them all! (Unless you're just laughing your way through saying, "This isn't for me.") I know you really want to be a virtuous wife and if you're not one already, you soon will be.

It won't be long now before those praises start pouring in. Of course, today, the way things are, you will probably hear a lot of jeers and put-downs long before you hear the praise. But rest assured, others are hearing those praises long before you do.

I wish this wasn't true, but, we, as a people, have gotten so far away from God and His plans and purposes, that we feel insecure and unsure of ourselves. It becomes hard to accept the good fortune of others. So, to cover up, we put on a smile and pull out the jokes, knowing how much they hurt us, but never thinking how much they hurt others.

This trend can be stopped! And will be stopped, by the virtuous wives and Biblical husbands of today. We can start by answering their cries with words of comfort and encouragement. Remember, he who hurts others with cruel jokes usually hurts worse than his object of hatred, so be kind. I'm not saying all jokes are bad, mainly those that cut to the bone.

When I read: Favor is deceitful, and beauty is vain, I think:

VANITY OF VANITIES, ALL IS VANITY. (Ecclesiastes 1:2)

VAIN, VAIN, BEAUTY IS VAIN. (Proverbs 31:31)

I don't believe God is telling us not to use makeup, not to dress nice, not to try to look our best, but, rather to be careful not to get caught up in the world's view of beauty and allow ourselves to be overcome by the flattery of one that is looking to deceive.

We must keep our priorities straight. God first, husband second, children third; people before things. Beauty last.

Remember, the virtuous wife is clothed in fine linen and purple. Is that the mark of a woman not clothed in beauty?

Esther had great beauty. It was that beauty that gave her favor in the King's eyes and opened the door for God to use her to save the Jews. How about Rachel, Rebecca, Ruth; just to name a few. Each were beautiful women. Each were used by God. When God talks about His bride, he talks of her adorning, her beauty.

To date, I haven't found much on makeup in the Bible. It does talk about Painting the eyes, so we know some woman did wear it. Many feel from what is said that it was a bad thing. Verses like:

Jeremiah 4:30

> **And when thou art spoiled, what wilt thou do? Though thou clothest thyself with crimson, though thou deckest thee with ornaments of gold, though thou rentest thy face with painting, in vain shalt thou make thyself fair; thy lovers will despise thee, they will seek thy life.**

To me that sounds more like, "Even though you do all these things, that won't change who you are." It wasn't the makeup that was bad, but the person. At this point in time, I don't feel confident in my knowledge on this topic to say if it is good, bad or indifferent. You will have to seek the Lord as to His direction for you. But, personally, right now, I really don't see anything wrong with it, if used correctly.

Fear the Lord, reverence Him; sing His praises all day long. Don't worry about rather you're getting the praises you deserve. If you concern yourself with yourself, you will become ugly and bitter. Fear (respect) the Lord and you will be praised.

So many say, "Life isn't fair!" But here God says, "Give her of the fruit of her hands." What could be fairer than that? What you give, you get. If you work, you receive, if you don't, you don't. You will be praised for what you do.

Other translations say:

> "...on (upon) her tongue." (YLT, SPRL. LAM)
>
> > Yea, I'm getting a little picky here, but there is a big difference between "on" and "in". If something is ON your hand, it could easily fall off, but if it is IN your hand, you have a much better grip on it. You will be less likely to lose it.
>
> "She surveyeth the ways of her household." (SPRL)
>
> > When you survey something, you take inventory of what is there, you don't add to or take from it. You do nothing for it. When you look after something you care for it, encourage it, add to it, enhance it.
>
> "Her children rise up and call her happy (blessed)." (RHM, RSV & BER)
>
> > A new nickname perhaps?
>
> "Her sons congratulate her..." (MOF)
>
> > Why not her daughters? Congratulations on doing a fine job...raising them? Thank-you, maybe, but congratulations?

Instead of "Favor is deceitful and beauty is vain":

"Comeliness is deceitful." (ABPS)

Comeliness is talking about your looks; well favor is more about actions. "You have obtained favor", not "you are favor."

"Beauty is breath" (BER)

I couldn't believe this one, so I looked it up to see if I was missing something. Breath = Life; Vain=empty, worthless. One of those has to be wrong! Guess which one.

"Beauty is passing" "Charms may wane, beauty wither" (BER, MOF, & NEB)

So, it's not deceptive or worthless, it just doesn't last?

I pray this book has been a blessing to you, and helped you become more of a blessing to your family.

When we go home to be with the Lord, we will be met at those pearly gates and receive praises for what we have done. If we do our own thing, there won't be much praise waiting for us. BUT, if we do as the Lord has commanded, we will hear, "Well done, good and faithful servant. Enter into the joy of the Lord."

Appendix I

ANSWERS TO DISCUSSION 1

1. Should we try to be the virtuous wife spoken of here?

If you don't try you will never attain. A virtuous wife has many great qualities we should all be striving to achieve.

2. What does being a virtuous wife entail?

To be humble, righteous, good, God-fearing, submissive (to God & husband), live morally. Everything detailed in these eight discussions and more.

3. How much are rubies worth?

The ruby is highly prized as a gemstone and is usually recognized as one of the three most precious gems, the others being the diamond and the emerald. Precious gems get better with age. The polished and refined stone is worth more than an uncut one.

4. Is our price (value) as an average wife today worth even that, let alone more?

I don't think we could have gotten much worse. Women of today have become very self-centered. We are running day-in day-out, trying to find a place to fit in, never finding a spot that makes us truly happy. We do everything everyone tells us we have to do to be "fulfilled"; completely forgetting what God in His Word told us. Then we wonder why we don't enjoy life. The average woman today is like the uncut stone, needing refining and polishing. We can only receive the polish we need from God's Word.

5. Why is a *Virtuous* wife worth so much more?

A virtuous wife has been polished. She has taken the time to get alone with God and discover what He has for her. Good qualities are always worth more than material possessions. You can accomplish much for the Lord with the right attitude and Spirit. You are limited in what you can do with material possessions. Good qualities never wear out; instead, they get better with use. These qualities are the outcome of a polished and refined woman, who has discovered what God has been saying since the dawn of time.

6. Why is it important for Christian women to be the best wife...?

As Christians we should always be striving to be the best, we can be at everything we do, we are after all, God's representatives on Earth. We should be setting the standard. The world will be watching us, along with our family, to see if our actions line up with our words. It is especially important if our husbands are not saved, since they will be won by our chaste conduct, not the continual naggings of a contentious wife.

7. When we change, what response can we expect from our husbands? Why?

Non-acceptance, rebuke, unbelief, totally negative. People don't like change, even good change. They get use to you the way you are and feel threatened when you change. Sometimes it's because they don't understand why you're changing, they think you are growing away from them, and they don't want to lose you.

Other times it's because they know they need to change too and aren't ready to do so. They want to know if this change in you will last, so they test you out to see. They hope you pass, but won't make it easy on you. If you pass, maybe there's hope for them. If you fail, there's no reason for them to try.

The test may be over in a week or may last several years. Remember, the way to win is through love and patience, not answering back with, "It would do you some good to make a few changes too." Love and accept them where they are. Do not point out their flaws, they already know them.

Our unsaved husband will likely either come to the Lord, or run as fast as he can. The conviction he feels will be great and it should be from the Lord, not from us.

8. What other spiritual laws will have a bearing on how he responds to you?

What ye sow, so shall ye reap. (2 Cor. 9:6)

Judge not, that ye be not judged. (Matt. 7:1)

God will not push himself on anyone (satan will)

You must/do serve a master either God or satan. (When it's satan, he will work against everything God stands for.)

9. Does this mean we're fighting a losing battle?

No, God made spiritual laws for our benefit. Man turned them against himself with his selfishness and disobedience. Once we know the score, we can fight anything. God will give us the victory, if we follow Him and His ways.

I CAN DO ALL THINGS THROUGH CHRIST, WHO STRENGTHENS ME!
Remember, this is talking about the things God gives us to do. NOT the things you put on yourself.

10. Is a gradual or overnight total, all at once change better? Why?

Gradual. An overnight change could scare them off. □ Actually, a gradual change is much easier to control and keep. If you try changing too much too fast, you could get overwhelmed and it could easily become too much to bear. You might give up before you've begun. We don't want that! But, on the other hand, don't go so slow that you and others can't see any progress. If you don't see progress, you are likely to give up.

Ch 1: WORD STUDIES

Wife:

Webster's 1828:

The lawful consort of a man; a woman who is united to a man in the lawful bonds of wedlock; the correlative of a husband …

Read and study the following scriptures:

- Gen. 2:20-25 – Women were made to be a helpmeet for men.

- Gen. 11:29-23:19; Heb. 11:11-12; I Pet. 3:1-6 - Sarah (Sarai)

- Gen. 24:1-67 – A good example of a woman leaving all she knows to be her husband's completely. He decides where you go, not you. (Yiks! Does that really still apply today?)

- Also study the many studies throughout this book on wives.

Virtuous:

Webster's 1828:

Morally good; acting in conformity to the moral law; practicing the moral duties, and abstaining from vice; ... Being in conformity to the moral or divine law; ... Chaste; *applied to women,* Efficacious by inherent qualities; as virtuous herbs; virtuous drugs (not in use)

Read and study these scriptures:

- Book of Ruth
- Prov. 12:4
- Phil. 4:8
- II Pet. 1:2-10

Love: Webster's 1828:

"In a general sense to be pleased with; to regard with affection, on account of some qualities which excite pleasing sensations or desire of gratification. ... We love our parents and children, on account of their connection with us, and on account of many qualities which please us. ... In short, we love whatever gives us pleasure and delight whether animal or intellectual; and if our hearts are right, we love God above all ... It is opposed to hatred. ... love is ardent friendship, or strong attachment springing from good will and esteem, and the pleasure derived from the company, civilities and kindnesses of others. ..."

Study these Scriptures:

Ex. 20:1-17	John 14:15	I John 4:6-5:3
Luke 6:26	Romans 5:6-8	II John
Luke 7:41-50	Romans 13:8-10	
John 13:33-35	I Corinthians 13	

Marriage:

Webster's 1828:

"The act of uniting a man and women for life; wedlock, the legal union of a man and woman for life. Marriage is a contract both civil and religious, by which the parties engage to live together, in mutual affection and fidelity, till death shall separate them. Marriage was instituted by God himself for the purpose of preventing the promiscuous intercourse of the sexes, for promoting domestic felicity and for securing the maintenance and education of children."

Study these Scriptures:

Gen 2:21-25	Roman 7:1-3	Eph 5:1-12
Matt 19:5-9	I Cor 7: 1-17	Hebrews 13:
Mark 19:5-9	Gal 5:14-26	

ANSWERS TO DISCUSSION 2

1. Can you force your husband to trust you?

No. But then, we're not out to force anything on anyone. It is our job to be a woman who can be trusted. If your husband refuses to trust anyone, then that is a problem beyond your control. Pray about it! Let God deal with him. Meanwhile, continue to be a loving supportive, submissive and trustworthy wife.

2. What are some things you can do to show that you can be trusted?

- Be truthful in everything you do and say.
- Do everything you can to make your home the best place to be.
- Do not over spend the budget. Save money whenever/ wherever you can.

Be a woman of your word. If you say you'll be home by ten, be home by ten; even if he comes home way past the time, he says he will. Or if something comes up, call to let him know why you will be late. This is not a rule just for children, it is common courtesy for all.

3. How do our husbands "Spoil"?

By overly pampering him, treating him like a child instead of your husband. You can damage his character by being ill tempered, sassy, arrogant, bossy or otherwise un-virtuous.

4. What good can you do your husband?

- Never put him down. He needs you to lift him up.
- SHOW your love, care and concern.
- Do things he likes. Be pleasing to his eye.
- Keep the house in order.

Speak well of him at all times and do not allow others to speak ill of him. That's like saying you agree with what they are saying.

ANSWERS TO DISCUSSION 3

1. What is the significance (Characteristics) of wool and flax?

Wool: Warm, Soft, (comfortable) Strong (stands up well)

Flax: Strong thread (holds things together) made from a plant with clusters of blue, white and pink flowers. (Strength in a pretty package.)

Even the colors have a meaning of their own:

- Blue: cool, refreshing
- Pink: to me stands for woman; it's a delicate color, soft. It is also a lighter shade of red, red meaning hot would make pink warm, comforting
- White: purity, clean

2. How can we apply the characteristics of wool & flax to ourselves?

We should keep ourselves well groomed; clean, neat, sensibly dressed. We should be warm, friendly and loving to others. Treat family like guests and guests like family. We should be soft, gentle, easy going.

All this beauty should be the covering for the strength within. We need to be as strong as an ox to stand against attacks of all types. We should remain "cool" under pressure.

3. Why is strength important for a wife?

A woman needs physical strength just to get through an average day of pushing brooms, mopping, vacuuming, cleaning, cooking and shopping. (Carrying those bags in two and three at a time can build up those muscles pretty fast.) Then when you add to that; carrying a baby for nine months before birth and another two or three years after, you can see where physical strength is very important for a woman.

4. Where do we get inner strength?

The Lord, reading His Word daily

Keeping in constant contact through prayer

Staying in fellowship with other believers

Praise and worship

5. As long as we do everything that's expected of us, is that enough?

No, if you do it because it's expected or because you have to, you will not be happy. Those around you will pick up on your mood and soon the whole house will be filled with gloom, probably no one will know why. Each day you will feel worse, and they will feel worse; an endless vicious circle that will seem unbreakable.

You will find it harder and harder to do the things you have to do and will never find the time for the things you want to do. Life will become drudgery and you won't care if you do anything or not.

6. What kind of attitude should you have?

One of willingness; a desire to please out of love. Even the most undesirable job won't seem so bad. You'll get done faster and have more time for things you enjoy. You'll be happy. Those around you will be happy. The fighting and bickering will stop. It may take a while, but it will stop.

ANSWERS TO DISCUSSION 4

1. How should we be shopping for food today?

Check/compare sales, coupons, brand name or store brand (Most store brands are brand name rejects because they weren't cut right or some other minor thing that doesn't affect taste or quality. Some store brands are pretty bad, so if you haven't yet, compare and see for yourself.)

Know your store; when they get new shipments in, find out what they add to their meats, etc. Check local farms and farm stores or co-ops. When possible, shop in bulk and freeze.

2. Is it necessary to get up early and make a good breakfast?

Yes, it has been a long time since they have eaten and a good breakfast starts them off right. It also starts your day off together, before heading off in separate directions. In this world of "You do your thing and I'll do mine". That is important.

That being said, I know some times it isn't possible. As I said in the last chapter, my first husband didn't want to take time to eat. My present husband doesn't often eat breakfast. We can't force them to do so. But, it is still an important meal and we should try to have a family breakfast whenever possible.

If your husband doesn't want to join you; you and the children can still eat together before they go to school or whatever the day holds.

3. Is this section dealing only with food for the body?

No, God rarely talks about food for the body without talking about food for the soul. Spiritual food is much more important. Be sure to give your family a good supply of His Word every day. Teach them how to fill up on Jesus and His Spirit. Show them how important it is to have fellowship with their Heavenly Father.

4. So what should a family breakfast include?

It's a good time for at least a five-minute devotion. In an unequally yoked home this may not be possible, but try to at least get a spiritual prayer in for guidance through the day. But, if this is going to upset your husband, don't do it.

You want your children's time with the Lord to be peaceful and happy. It would be best to find a time when your husband isn't home. Remember, when the reception is cold, three words of love can mean more than three chapters from the Bible. Keep things on a happy note as much as possible

ANSWERS TO DISCUSSION 5

1. What is today's field to buy and plant?

   A literal field (acreage), a job opportunity, a special ability God has given you to "Plant your feet into." Search your field of interest, "Buy" into the idea that this IS your field, and plant your vineyard. Dig in and let the fruits grow.

2. What kind of fruit would you grow in your vineyard?

   If a field where grass can grow; whatever would grow best there. What you do the best with, what you and your family want, like and need.

   If a job-outside the home. (Keep in mind Titus 2:5 and all that is said in this chapter) do the best you can, get raises and promotions.

   If it's your home: it would be your family, house, meals you cook, things you do.

A home business- do your best work on every piece. A job well done is its own reward. It keeps your old customers and gets you new ones.

3. In evaluating your abilities, what questions should you ask yourself?

   Do I like what I'm doing?

   Is it what God wants me to do? (You will find if it is what God wants you to do, you will enjoy doing it.)

   Is it good enough to sell (literally or figuratively to buyer, boss or family?)

   Am I satisfied with the quality? Will anyone else be?

   Can I trust my judgment of my work? (If not find someone you can trust for an honest assessment.)

4. What other kind of vineyard could she be planting?

   The second definition is: *Area of action, or field of endeavor, esp. one of a spiritual nature.*

   She could have bought land to use for homes for the homeless, or as training grounds for the unskilled. Perhaps, she could have started a Woman's Bible Study. The possibilities are almost endless.

5. Is it necessary to plan a daily exercise program?

   That depends on you; some people feel they need it and maybe they do. Others get plenty of exercise from their daily routine. Going up and down stairs, and chasing children are great for the heart. Pushing floor equipment, washing dishes and hanging clothes strengthens the arms.

If you feel you need an exercise program and can fit it into your schedule without infringing on your family, by all means do so. Just remember the key words:

WITHOUT INFRINGING ON YOUR FAMILY.

6. Should you be a workaholic?

   NO! You may stay up late working; because that's the time you have set aside for it. Your time has been divided up, God first, Family second, house third, job last. But God has given his beloved sleep. (Ps. 127:2)

ANSWERS TO DISCUSSION 6

1. Do you stretch out your hand to the poor and needy? Who are the needy?

The widow down the road, the older couple next door, the young mother without a car, a friend just out of the hospital, a family member fallen on hard times. How about the guy in need of a kidney, or the little boy who comes to your house because no one is home at his? How about the little girl that comes over to play and says, "I wish my mom and dad were more like you." How about her mom and dad?

Perhaps even the richest family in town? They are often the poorest; no true friends, always looking for ways to increase their riches but never having time for family and friends.

Then of course we have the ones we more commonly think of, that "dirty, smelly, drunken bum" living on the street. Do you pass these people by, because you're too busy, or if you help once they'll expect it again and again? "After all, God wouldn't want us to be taken advantage of."

Matt 5:39-44

But I say unto you, That ye resist not evil: but whosoever shall smite thee on thy right cheek, turn to him the other also. And if any man will sue thee at the law, and take away thy coat, let him have thy cloak also. And whosoever shall compel thee to go a mile, go with him twain. <u>Give to him that asketh thee, and from him that would borrow of thee turn not thou away.</u> Ye have heard that it hath been said, Thou shalt love thy neighbour, and hate thine enemy. <u>But I say unto you, Love your enemies, bless them that curse you, do good to them that hate you, and pray for them which despitefully use you, and persecute you;</u>

2. In what ways, in and out of the home, can we help?

Send/give money food clothing direct to them or to organizations that help them. (Check them out! Some organizations pocket more than they use for the purpose at hand. God calls us to be good stewards with His money.)

Make and deliver meals.

Take them on errands or offer to pick up what they need.

Do laundry, sewing, mending, cleaning, babysitting, etc.

Share our Faith, be a friend.

3. What should your attitude be while serving in these ways?

Humble, concerned, but not patronizing or superior. Loving, kind, servant, as unto the Lord. It should be done in secret, not to gain man's praise:

Matthew 6:1-4

Take heed that ye do not your alms before men, to be seen of them: otherwise ye have no reward of your Father which is in heaven. Therefore when thou doest thine alms, do not sound a trumpet before thee, as the hypocrites do in the synagogues and in the streets, that they may have glory of men. Verily I say unto you, They have their reward. But when thou doest alms, let not thy left hand know what thy right hand doeth: That thine alms may be in secret: and thy Father which seeth in secret himself shall reward thee openly.

4. Why should we reach out?

We are commanded to in:

Acts 20:28 Take heed therefore unto yourselves, and to all the flock, over the which the Holy Ghost hath made you overseers, to feed the church of God, which he hath purchased with his own blood. KJV

Rom 12:20-21

Therefore if thine enemy hunger, feed him; if he thirst, give him drink: for in so doing thou shalt heap coals of fire on his head. Be not overcome of evil, but overcome evil with good. KJV

I always thought this was kind of a negative thing. A way to pay back your enemy for what he did to you. But it is a positive thing.

It comes from a time when one family kept a fire for the whole community. When the coals were hot, they would put them into a basket and place the basket on their head. (They wrapped a large towel over their head so it would not burn) Then carried it to the other families.

The coals would keep them warm while they went to deliver them to others. Perhaps, even warming his own personality.

Spiritually, heaping coals of fire on your enemy warms his heart and changes his way of thinking. Fire is symbolic of love. Warm your enemy with your love; melt his heart with the warmth of your love.

Info gleaned from: Eastern Customs and Idioms of the Bible. The Teachings of Orientalisms By Bishop K.C. Pillai

Luke 14:13-14

13 But when thou makest a feast, call the poor, the maimed, the lame, the blind: 14 And thou shalt be blessed; for they cannot recompense thee: for thou shalt be recompensed at the resurrection of the just. KJV

To get outside of ourselves, forget our problems, allowing God to solve them.

ANSWERS TO DISCUSSION 7

1. Significance of: a) Scarlet b) rich c) tapestry d) linen e) silk f) purple?

Scarlet – Escalate- rich cloth, bright red color.

Rich – Deep, full, warm, Elegant, sumptuous, extravagant.

Tapestry – Heavy decorated fabric.

Linen – Lustrous durable fabric woven from flax.

Silk – Fine soft thread, cloth made of silk

Purple – Symbol of royalty or high rank

2. How should we apply these Qualities to ourselves, our marriage, our family?

We should always be striving to be the best we can be. Our lives should be rich, full of all that we can do. Fill your home first with love, then the things that interest your family. If you're not blessed with decorator talent, find someone with your tastes, that can give you some ideas and maybe help you in achieving the finished product of your choice.

Be leery of the pros, they tend to want to do things their way and charge you big for it. If you have the money and want to use a professional, make sure he will do it your way.

Extravagance doesn't always mean expensive, expensive isn't always best. Be extravagant in doing, not in buying. You can give the air of royalty without having the title or living in a palace.

Nor, should you have a superior attitude. But rather, it is the royalty we have through Christ sharing His inheritance with us. Therefore, we should act as He did; loving, kind, giving, caring and sharing ...SERVANT.

3. Why spend all that money on tapestry and linen?

Tapestry is heavy. It helps keep out the cold in winter and heat in summer. It helps conserve energy. Very smart wife; pay a little more now, a lot less later.

Linen is very durable. It will last a long time. Again, it may be more expensive, but it pays for itself with use.

Who we are in Christ is who we are. People need to know about our royal inheritance. BUT, with these priestly robes comes an attitude of humility. We must never let ourselves get caught up in the high position and start acting as though we were better than anyone else. Remember, our inheritance came through Christ and He was servant to all.

4. What can you do to enhance your husband's standing with the elders?

They will know you by your fruits, the Bible says. So, keep your faith pure and strong. Do what is right at all times and word will get around that your husband has found a woman of true and great value.

5. If we want to help add to the family income, do we have to make things to sell?

This lady was very successful with what she did. She had a great talent for sewing. Not everyone has that. She would not sell inferior products. If someone were to try to sell something they didn't have the talent for, it would be inferior and therefore, should not be sold.

All women possess a special talent that they can capitalize on. It may not have anything to do with sewing, crafts, or sales, but you can be sure it is exactly what your family needs. It is up to you to pray and seek God, to find out what it is.

6. How can we rejoice in times to come?

A woman who does all this is organized. If you are organized and following God's plan for your life, you can do all this and much, much more. You will be rejoicing because you will see your life coming into focus. You will see your family coming together. You will have true joy that only God can give you.

ANSWERS TO DISCUSSION 8

1. Where do you get wisdom?

It is a gift of God. You obtain it by reading His Word.

2. What is the law of kindness?

Ephesians 4:32

And be ye kind one to another, tenderhearted, forgiving one another, even as God for Christ's sake hath forgiven you.

3. Do we have to stay home in order to be a good mother?

There are many good mothers who work outside the home. But, this book is not about just being a good wife and mother; it is about doing things God's way.

4. You don't have to be right there all the time to be watching over them. Right?

Here it says, "She watches over the ways of her household." How can you watch if you're not with them? No, you can't be with them 24 hrs. a day, but you do need to make home and family your priority, with only God ahead of them. (That's God, not church or ministry. Although both are important and should not be ignored.)

5. What is "Bread of Idleness"?

It's what some of the women in the work force think the women at home are eating/doing. Of course, you and I know better. It's what you do when you have nothing else to do. Being idle, by Biblical standards, is a sin.

God doesn't want His children to be idle, because when you have nothing to do, you lose site of the truth and begin to gossip, along with many other things that shouldn't be done.

6. Why are charm and beauty so bad?

Because they are only skin deep. It's what's inside, that matters. When you rely on your charm and beauty you become selfish, greedy and conceited.

7. Why will a woman who fears the Lord be praised over one who doesn't fear the Lord?

We receive praise for what we do for the Lord, as He directs us. Nothing done by our own power, or initiative, will last. Only what's done by God's power will make eternity. The things of Earth mean nothing and count for nothing.

Appendix II

Key to other translations:

- AAT The Bible: An American Translation
- ABPS The Holy Bible Containing the Old and New Testaments: an Improved Edition (American Baptist Publication Society)
- ASV American Standard Version
- BAS Bible in Basic English
- BER Modern Language Bible: The new Berkley version in Modern English
- JERUS The Jerusalem Bible
- KNOX The Holy Bible a translation from the Latin Vulgate in the light of the Hebrew and Greek Originals (Monsignor Ronald Knox)
- LAM The Holy Bible from Ancient Eastern Manuscripts (George M. Lamsa)
- MOF A New Translation of the Bible (James Moffatt)
- NAB The New American Bible
- NEB The New English Bible
- RHM The Emphasized Bible: A New Translation (J.B. Rotherham)

- SPRL A Translation of the Old Testament Scriptures from the Original Hebrew (Helen Spurrell
- TAY The Living Bible Paraphrased (Kenneth TGaylor)
- YLT Young's Literal Translation of the Holy Bible (Robert Young)

The following books and booklets are excellent reading for more on this topic. Please if at all possible, get them and read them. If you can't find them at your local Christian Bookstore, try these addresses. The prices may be old, so call or write for current pricing or bulk rates for your group study.

1) FAR ABOVE RUBIES $1
COST PER BOOK/BOOKLET
BY NOLDA Flamagan
P. O. BOX 397
Whitesboro, TX 76273

2) THE WOMAN'S ROLE $.50
BY DR. CURTIS HUTSON
SWORD OF THE LORD PUBLISHING
P. O. BOX 1099
MURFREESBORO, TN 37133
800-243-9673 615-848-6943
FAX 615-848-6943
E-MAIL 102657.3622@CUMPUSERVE.COM

3) <u>WOMEN AND CHURCH MINISTRY</u>
BY NATHANIEL WEST
CHRISTIAN FELLOWSHIP
11000 SANDPIT ROAD
ALEXANDER, NY 14005
716-591-0031

4) <u>ME? OBEY HIM?</u> $3.95
BY ELIZABETH RICE HANDFORD
SWORD OF THE LORD PUBLISHER
(SEE ABOVE)

5) THE DIVINE ROMANCE BY DR. BRIAN SIMMONS & GRETCHEN RODRIGUEZ, PUBLISHED BY BROADSTREET PUBLISHING.

For a better understanding of the way the Bible would have been understood by the people it was originally written to:
6) ISRAEL BIBLE CENTER
DR. ELI LIZORKIN-EYZENBERG
HTTPS://ISRAELBIBLECENTER.COM/

Leader's Guide

Here you will find a few helpful suggestions on how to use this book more productively. I have broken it down by chapters so you can read each section before doing its corresponding chapter.

If you are leading a group, I would suggest you plan on 17 weeks to do this book. That will give you one week to describe what the book is about, go through the introduction and ask any basic questions to set the stage for a good workout.

Perhaps you could have a lady's tea and invite all the ladies from your church. (If you really feel energetic, you could invite ladies from other churches and give them the idea to take home to their church.)

That leaves you two weeks per chapter. Some chapters may only take one week; others may take three or more. Don't rush through the book to finish it in the 17 weeks, instead take as much time as you need, to get the most from it.

I also highly recommend four other booklets to go with this study. "Far Above Rubies" by Nolda Flamagan, "The Woman's Role" by Curtis Hutson, "Woman and Church Ministry" by Nathaniel West and the book, "Me Obey Him?" by Elizabeth Rice Handford. Information on these can be found in Appendix II

1st Week:

This is the time to explain what you will be doing, and get a firm commitment from everyone to be at all the meetings and "WORK" the book. If they just want to read it, they can do that on their own time. This group study is for the women who want to improve their life and become the women God wants them to be.

If you, the leader, have taken this class before, you should, if possible, keep your prayer partner from that class. She can help you with new problems that may come up in this class. Start this class with an even number of women, but if there is an odd number interested and you can't find another, put your name in and get a prayer partner for this class.

If you have not taken the class, you will be working the book same as everyone else. If adding your name would make it an odd number, then find yourself a prayer partner outside the class. (If you have taken it, still work the book again, you can improve on things you slacked off on, or didn't quite get the first time.)

If you have decided on the tea, pick a theme, "Victorian Tea Time", "Country Neighbors", "Virtuous Wives of Tomorrow Today" "your own idea", and decorate accordingly. If you have decided to invite other churches, allow enough time for them to get the invitation and fit the tea into their schedule.

Planning some special music to be played before you begin would help get people organized and settled early. (And if you're running a bit late, it won't be so quickly noticed.)

Perhaps your pastor would like a chance to say a few words before turning the meeting over to the one who will be leading the class.

Following, is a brief outline you may want to adhere to for this first meeting, rather you do the tea or not. Remember this is your show. Do it your way.

1. Welcome: If you have guests tell a little about your church, Pastor, services/times etc.

2. Pastor's welcome: If he wants to be included, don't insist that he do this. He is after all one of the busiest people in the church. If he doesn't, perhaps his wife will.

3. Talk a little about missions, how your church has started this new mission outreach to women and how other churches represented here today could too. Add some Scripture relevant to how you see the ministry.

4. Tell a little about yourself and why you chose this as your mission field

5. You may or may not want to use my testimony at this time. Being it borders on areas covered in the book it may give too much information and be better read when you finish the book.

6. Introduce book: You may not agree with everything in this book, but I don't believe you will find any of it to be unbiblical or unloving in the approach to those "touchy" subjects. One thing that really impressed me was the wide range of subjects these nine verses cover. They actually touch on every aspect of your life. If you really want to know what being a wife, mother, friend, missionary and Christian is all about, read this book. It's all here. It can truly change your life.

7. Explain how your meetings will be run and approximately how many weeks you're talking about.

8. Read the dedication and "A little about this book..." (Explain how the book is broken down; show the book, so they can see how easy it is to follow.)

9. Read the broken-down version of the Scripture. (Pages 3 & 4)

10. Read the prescription

11. Answer any questions

12. Get a show of hands of those who think this sounds like something they would like to study. Send a signup sheet around for the women in your church, or who are not affiliated with any church, that would like to take the class. (If someone from another church wants to take the class with you that is up to them and you, but don't give any the impression that you are out to steal sheep.)

13. Explain how those from other churches can get copies of the book.) If you have enough, you could offer them one to take with them.)

14. End your meeting. Have someone at the back of the room that can answer questions for those who are leaving. Also, if you have books available for them, they can be handed out

there. If your church is real mission orientated, and have the funds to do so, you could give a book to everyone who comes. Or, you could have some available for those who want to buy one. Either way, you could give them information on where they can purchase the book should they decide to do so later.

15. Ask those that want to take the class with you to stay a few more minutes.

16. Take a five-minute break for those who are leaving to get to the back of the room.

17. Explain prayer partners and pick them.

18. Hand out books and their homework assignments. (Explain payment arrangements for the book) Homework: evaluations, questions for chapter 1, word studies – "Virtuous" "Wife" "marriage" and "Love" and first two virtuous wife studies – Eve & Noah's wife & daughters-in-law. Caution them not to cheat by looking at my answers. My answers are examples and only

give part of the picture there are many other things that should be added that are equally important.

19. Decide on meeting day & time. You may want to wait two weeks for your next meeting, to give time to get the evaluations done.

20. Say good-by & thank everyone for coming

21. clean up

Additional thoughts on picking prayer partners and what they should do:

Hand out a small piece of paper to everyone. Have them write their name and phone number on the paper. When you get them back, divide them evenly between two hats, boxes, or some other container. Draw a name from each and those two will be prayer partners. Continue drawing until everyone has been paired. As you call their names, have them come forward to get their partners info. Write (or have someone else do this for you.) their names down on a piece of paper so you will have a list of the prayer partners. (Don't worry about phone numbers, you should have that on the signup sheet.)

While the paper is being handed out, the info gathered, and sent back, explain what it is for: "We are going to draw for prayer partners. Now, I know I could let you choose your own partners, but then you would choose your best friend and that may not be who God wants you with. So, we're going to let him choose, by drawing two names from a hat. He can determine what two get put together.

"Your prayer partner is key to your success with this study. (For those reading this book on your own, find a prayer partner. Try to convince her to do the study with you, or on her own at the same time. THIS IS VERY IMPORTANT. The more serious you are with what you read, the more important this will be.)

"Before leaving today/night set up a time to get together with your partner within the next two or three days. Allow one to three hours, this will be the only time you will need to do this, (but maybe not the only time you will want to.)

"Before you get together, go over the evaluation form. Pray about it, then on separate sheets of paper, answer each of the questions as honestly as you can for you, and your partner. Obviously, if you just met her tonight you won't be able to answer them for her.

"Remember, these evaluation forms are guidelines. They won't have everything you need to work on, so add anything else you think of. As we go through the study, you will be adding more.

"When you meet with your partner, pray together about the work you have ahead of you. Then, get yourselves a cup of herb tea and set at the kitchen table to go over your lists together. As you discuss the questions, you will get to know each other a little better. Combine ideas and thoughts, with the Spirit's guidance, to come up with a revised list for each of you.

"From this form, make a list of areas you need to work on throughout this study. In the order you NEED to, not necessarily WANT to work on them. The Spirit will help you decide the order.

"Devise your plan of attack. See the sample as a guide to making these lists. As you start working your plan, you may realize you don't have the order quite right. It's okay to change the order AFTER praying alone and with your partner. I caution though, be sure God is telling you to change the order, not your own fear or your desire to avoid something right now.

"Also, as you go through the book you will probably be adding to your list. This is a good thing. It means your growing wiser. However, don't let the list overwhelm you. It is there to help you organize what you need to work on. That way you can work on the first things first, while putting the rest on the back burner, without forgetting them, until you're ready to work on them.

"As you go through your lists you may come to some you have already mastered while working on others. Another sign that you are becoming the Virtuous wife you want to be.

"Set a time that will be good for both of you to call each day. A time that doesn't interfere with either family's activities. Decide who will call, and if you have children at home try to have something for them to do so you will be uninterrupted. Easy to say, I know. (Been there, done that.) This call should be kept short and to the business at hand. It is for edification, uplifting encouragement and prayer, not the latest gossip of the day.

"If the call is not made when expected, this may indicate the need to pray for your partner and what she is going through right then. But, don't let the day go by without a call to see that she is alright.

"Find out what the day holds for your partner, (if you've decided to make this call in the evening, what the next day holds.) What areas she's struggling with the most, what triumphs she had the day before, etc. Remember your specific goals; short- and long-range; not "to become a virtuous wife" but rather what you need to do to attain that goal.

"Then, pray for the Lord's guidance and blessing for that (or the next) day and for any specific problems, you're encountering. Are these the goals God has for you today? Be sure you're following His agenda; not yours. This shouldn't take more than 5-15 minutes. DO NOT talk about anything else at this time. Not even Church business or other spiritual matters.

"If you need to talk about anything else, do so on a separate call. This is very important. If you start talking about other things you will forget the more important business at hand, and satan will steal something good and turn it to evil. Don't let him. This is not a gab session; don't waste each other's time.

"As a prayer partner, you are not only committing to finishing the book and becoming a virtuous wife, you are also committing to helping your partner finish the book and both of you becoming virtuous wives. Pray for her and her family daily in your personal prayers.

"As you seek direction for you, seek for her too. You are there to help keep her balanced. Don't let her move ahead to fast, nor lag behind. Remember, when you take on a prayer partner, you take on her family; they are part of her.

"If she's being too hard on herself, remind her of the improvements she's already made. If she's not trying hard enough, give her a gentle and loving push. You are to hold each other accountable before the Lord.

"Decide your daily schedules together and when you call the next day, you'd better say, "I accomplished all we planned." If you don't, you'd better have a really good reason; NOT excuse, why you didn't.

"The only good reason is "God changed my plans, by sending an unexpected interruption." Remember, If God gave you the schedule, He will have already built-in time for the unexpected interruption, because He knew it was coming.

"If you see something in her life that you think needs correcting, don't go to her, go to God. Seek Him for the right way to approach the topic, IF you should approach the topic.

"If after much praying you feel God has shown this to you because He wants you to go to her, do so very gently and lovingly. Tell her what she needs to hear, not necessarily what YOU THINK she needs to hear.

"Be sure to listen! Don't assume that since you saw this you have all the answers. Don't assume anything. Things are not always what they appear. If she does something you think is wrong, find out why she did it. She may be more right than you think.

"Keep everything said in total confidence. No one else needs to know your partners struggles. If she wants them known, she can tell them herself.

"No matter how tempting it may be, do not get ahead of yourself. God gave us a specific order to follow. He knows best, so stick to His divine order. As you read each chapter, refer back to that Ch. Discussion.

"Some areas I've enlarged on, others are pretty much self-encompassing and I've tried not to repeat myself too much. So, if it is repeated, it is most likely VERY important."

1st Chapter

As with all future chapters, break wherever you need to. Some chapters are long and you may need two or three meetings to get through them.

I like to open studies with prayer, praise and worship. 15 minutes to ½ hour for this step is usually good for a women's study, but sometimes the Spirit will say otherwise. As with all areas of Church life we should let the Spirit direct.

Ch 1 is a little different than the rest. Some of the things given to do in the beginning will take most of the book to finish, (maybe longer) This is a quick overview of things to work on. I don't expect anyone to perfect everything in one week, but all should work on it until you complete it. (Some of this is what we gave for homework at the first meeting.)

In my outline, I have you reading each chapter as part of the class time. You could instead, give it as homework and only discuss it in class.

a. Discuss answers to discussion one.

   b. Q. 4 If you were able to get them, hand out booklet "Far above Rubies" read and discuss.

2. Read and discuss Ch. 1 together

   a. Discuss word studies as you read, when they come up

3. Do mini studies on Virtuous Women. (Some of the women in the Bible are not very virtuous. Discuss them anyway. See where they went wrong and what they could have done instead.)

4. Homework:

   a. Do the next two Virtuous Women (V.W.)- Sarai & Rebeckah (if you spend two weeks or more on a chapter, you could do two women each week. The rest of these suggestions would be split between the two weeks or however long you spend on the chapter.)

   b. List your contentious habits

   c. List corrective measures to take for above

   d. Practice "Biting your tongue"

   e. Put secret "Honey do list" or method that works for you and your husband into action

   f. Discussion 2

5. Questions, Pray, dismiss

Chapter 2

1. Discuss answers to Discussion 2
2. Read & discuss Ch 2
3. Discuss this week's V.W. studies
4. Homework:
    a. Keep working previous assignments
    b. V.W. – Moses' mother & Sister-Miriam(Or whatever two are next)
    c. Discussion 3
    d. Watch your tongue
    e. Be an encourager

Chapter 3

1. Discuss answers to discussion 3
2. V. W. studies
3. Read & discuss Ch. 3,
4. Homework:
    a. Keep working on previous assignments
    b. Word study on Love

c. V. W. –next two

d. Start reading Song of Solomon

e. Write out your cleaning schedule – pre & Spring Cleaning

   i. Decide the order you want to tackle the rooms in, not how long it will take.

f. Discussion 4

Chapter 4

1. Discussion 4 questions
2. V. W. Studies
3. Read & discuss Ch. 4
4. Discuss the possibility of starting a bartering system in your church
5. Homework:

   a. Previous assignments

   b. Keep reading Song of Solomon

   c. V.W.-

   d. Start studying on health issues – herbal vers drug medicine, natural vers synthetic vitamins & herbs; whole grain vers "Enriched" grains etc.

e. If your group has decided to start a bartering system, make out your lists

    i. If you are the organizer - write out a church announcement & list of rules. Talk with Pastor (Be sure he is okay with the idea). If you're going to utilize a bulletin board, get it ready.

f. Discussion 5

Chapter 5

1. Discuss Discussion 5
2. V. W. Studies
3. Read & discuss Ch. 5
4. If you were able to get them hand out booklets: "Women's Role" & "Women in Church Ministry" read at home, discuss as group at next meeting
5. Homework:
    a. Previous assignments
    b. Song of Solomon
    c. V.W.

d. With new information on fields, re-answer questions 1 & 2

e. Discussion 6

f. Read Women's Role; & Women in Church Ministry

Chapter 6

1. Discuss discussion 6
2. V.W. Studies
3. Read & discuss Ch. 6
4. Discuss books Women's Role & Women in Church Ministry.

Homework:

a. Previous assignments

b. V. W.

c. Write your love story Song of Solomon style

d. Put Luke 14:13-14 into practice

e. Put the gleaning principle into effect. (If you don't have a garden, let them glean other things – household items, food items from your cupboards, your talents/ knowledge; teach them something you know.)

f. If you haven't finished your pre-spring cleaning and started spring cleaning yet, you should be doing so this week.

g. Discussion 7

h. Start reading "Me Obey Him" by Elizabeth Rice Handford

Chapter 7

1. Discuss discussion 7

2. V. W. studies

3. Read & discuss Ch 7

4. Homework:

- Try to finish up past assignments

- V. W.

- Start thinking about a home business. What talents could you put to use? Get your husband's input. Be sure your house is in order before putting a lot of time into the business. You don't want to lose what you've gained.

- Discussion 8

- Consider reading your version of Song of Solomon to your husband.

Chapter 8

1. Discuss discussion questions
2. Discuss V. W. study
    a. Read & discuss Ch. 8
3. If you did not read my testimony at the beginning you may want to read it now.
4. Homework:
    a. Finish all extra studies (VW studies will be an on-going thing for the rest of the year or two or three... □)
    b. Start home business & home ministry if acceptable to your husband. You may not be ready to start the home business for several months after finishing this book. But you could start planning what you will do and how to do it.
    c. Keep studying all the women of the Bible. Then move into women from our church history and other great women of faith. Glean all you can from their lives. (This could be a life time endeavor.)
    d. Keep your home in order.
    e. Keep involved with your family and friends
    f. Stay close to God
    g. REJOICE!!!

- Leader: Plan a meal for your last week. Make it a special time of rejoicing. Something special for all the hard work everyone has done.

Personal Testimony

When the Lord first gave me the Titus 2 ministry, I remembered the different churches I'd been in, and all the "older women" I met and fellowshipped with. I said, "But, Lord, I can't do this now, I still have children in school therefore, I'm still in the younger women stage. Then He gave me another way to look at it.

I started talking with the older women in our church and found most had been with the Lord nine to fifteen years. I was raised in the church. I don't remember a time without Him, but one week remains very clear to me.

I had been reading the Word and praying before going to bed for several years, but one night, I asked myself, "Have I ever asked Jesus into my heart?" I wasn't sure, so I decided it was time to make sure and I did so that night. The next night I didn't feel any different, so I asked Him again, and the next night, and the next, until He said, "You only have to ask once."

I was eight or nine at that time, so, at age 31, that meant I was over 22 years old in Christ. At least five years older than anyone in my church, even, I dare say, the Pastor. I guess that qualified me to be one of the "older women".

BUT ... that doesn't mean I have all the answers, or by any means have perfected the walk of faith. I still have a lot to learn and a long way to go. (Even now, over thirty years later, there is always more to learn.)

In addition, the pastor had given me this life verse when I joined the church:

Titus 2:3The aged women likewise, that *they be* in behaviour as becometh holiness, not false accusers, not given to much wine, teachers of good things; 4That they may teach the young women to be sober, to love their husbands, to love their children, 5*To be* discreet, chaste, keepers at home, good, obedient to their own husbands, that the word of God be not blasphemed.

Can you imagine in a day when women run the home, church, work place and government; being called to teach submission! That a woman is to be a keeper at home. NOT in the House and Senate, as so many like to say, but AT HOME.

But wait, it gets worse. They also are to OBEY their HUSBANDS. WHAT? They can't be the ones wearing the paints? Oh, NO! This is not an easy calling!

But, as I studied submission, I came to see the beauty, the love, the peace. Still, I find it hard to convince others of this. Even the men don't want to hear it! Could it be, they know, that with their wife's submission comes their higher calling to love their wife AS Christ Loves the church?

Of course, both need to remember, their obedience to the Word is not dependent on another's obedience to it. But, I will never give up trying, for it is a truth that those willing to see will embrace with thanksgiving.

Several years have passed since I first wrote this book. Many things have changed. My two oldest children are married with children of their own. I have a new husband and I now get up between 5 and 6 a.m. (Sometimes even earlier than that.)

Yes, I have finally succeeded in occasionally getting up before the sun! I no longer stay up till 2 or 3 in the morning. (Well, maybe occasionally ☺) My new husband prefers that I go to bed with him. (I prefer that too.)

I know this book will raise many questions, probably top among them is, "Do you REALLY believe and follow all of this?" The answers are "Yes", and "I try to, but many times I do fall short of the mark."

I also have been tested in it many times, especially when it comes to working. It's easy to say, "let go and let God." But when it comes to having your source of income totally cut out, with the bills still pouring in and no possible means of paying them in sight, it gets difficult, to say the least. Living by faith is a nice ideal, but when you get tested in it, it isn't always easy.

When every home-based business you try gets stopped, because you don't have the start-up money, you start rethinking your stand and start asking, "Lord, am I right on this issue?"

Add to this, everyone telling you, you need to get a job, and having your ex-husband telling your children that you are lazy, that's why you're not working. (Even though he owes you enough in back child support and alimony to buy a house with cash and refuses to pay.)

Yes, you start questioning, "Am I really right?" It would be so much easier to get a job. But, do you do what the world says? Or do you do what God is telling you?

Yes, I did say ex-husband. I'm sure most everyone remembers a comment I made in the beginning of this book. When talking about trust in marriage, I said, "Despite what the world says, you can't just go out and find another one" (Meaning spouse).

There are times God will allow divorce. But He still hates it. At the time, I first wrote this book, I believed there was no grounds for marrying someone else while your first spouse was still alive. Marriage is a lifetime commitment, until death.

If you mix salt and water, can you ever have fresh water or just salt again? Only, if the water dies. When the water evaporates the salt is left whole and complete. But until the water dies, they are whole and complete only when together. They cannot be separated.

And that is what God say's about a man and his wife. They cannot be separated except by death. For three years after our divorce, I clung to that; and refused to even consider marrying someone else; while, he was alive; even though my husband had done so.

All my friends and pastors kept telling me, "You didn't do anything wrong. Why should you have to suffer? God doesn't want you to be alone for the rest of your life."

My only answer, although I didn't tell them this, was, "True, but then God didn't want me to marry him in the first place. That was my mistake. He knew what would happen. But, there are consequences for everything you do. Two wrongs do not make a right. Besides, I'm a lot happier now than I have been for a long time."

One night, three plus years after our divorce, the Lord told me to read I Cor. 7 again. When I got to, "He hath called us to peace." He told me to look up Peace in the Strong's Concordance. I had done this before at His prompting, but didn't get anything new from it.

This time I saw in the midst of a page of 6 pt fount these words jump off the page appearing as 18 pt fount:

"+ set at one again"

I found this interesting and confusing. For years, I studied this topic and every time I found something new, it always led to the affirmation, that marriage is until death no matter what. Now it seemed He was telling me, in this one case, He would make me whole and complete again by myself, without my husband dying.

Could that really be the case? I wondered if it had to do with the spiritual man being dead. I also wondered if my first husband had refused God too many times and he won't get another chance. I hope, for his sake, this is not the case, but I did very distinctly hear the

Lord tell me to stop praying for him. I had to be sure, then I read the verse again, substituting these words for peace.

1 Cor 7:15 But if the unbelieving departs, let him depart. A brother or a sister is not under bondage in such cases: but God hath called us to be set at one again. KJV-PJ revised □

I took another two or three weeks to study I Cor. 7 again. (Please read I Cor. 7:6-17) I still had many questions that I didn't want to ask, because to me there was only one answer and it wasn't the one I wanted. BUT, when all is said and done, I know God's way is the best way and I hope I will always follow it. This was my final conclusion:

- In the case of two Christian's getting a divorce NO REMARRIAGE!!
- In the case of a believer leaving his/her non-believing spouse NO RE-MARRIAGE!!
- In the case of the unbeliever leaving???? Do I dare hope that it is truly acceptable before the Lord? I am leaning in that direction, BUT I would not at this time counsel in that direction. The penalty for being wrong is toooo great; and even the experts disagree on this issue.

When all is said and done, we each must make our own decision. We are responsible before the Lord for what we do. If you are sure in your heart that you are right, Great! I sincerely hope you are. But, if you have any doubts, be careful!

Going back to the salt water analogy; there is one way to separate the two without either dying. If you heat the water and trap the steam transferring it to another pot, then, cool it off, turning it back into water, the salt will stay in the first pot.

Transferring this to marriage; when you have an unsaved spouse who makes life unbearable, he or she is adding the heat to the marriage, making the water steam then one of you has to leave, or one of you will end up dying.

According to I Cor. 7 If the believer leaves, he or she must remain unmarried, but if the unbeliever leaves, the believer is now "set at one again".

Yes, a few months after coming to this conclusion, I made the decision to re-marry. Was it the right one? I may never know in this life, but I do know this; I have never been happier.

My new husband loves and protects me like I never thought possible. He loves the Lord and wants to live his life for him. He stumbles a lot; it has been a rough road for him. He is stubborn, set in his ways, doesn't like to change; which causes its share of problems. But his heart is in the right place and he keeps working on the rough spots. Besides, I'm not perfect either.

For the first time, since the start of my first marriage, I truly feel safe and secure. I know I can trust him with anything. And yes, I truly love him in every way possible. No more living with just an Agrippa type love.

Don't get me wrong; we still have our problems. Money is still a big issue; bills keep coming in faster and bigger but the paychecks appear to be covering, although there isn't much left over. And even though he agreed with me that I should not be working outside the home, we still saw no other option for a while.

Is this a test, or is it God saying, "Times have changed the unacceptable is now a necessity"? I have always said, and still believe, Times may change, but God never does. His word remains true throughout time. So, if women were to be "keepers at home" when the Bible was written, they are still to be "Keepers at home" today. He will provide another way. And for us He did. Even though I did work outside the home for close to 15 years I never lost sight of my dream to come back home. I kept praying for it, knowing I did not belong where I was. And one day He provided the way.

My life has been full of trials, tribulations and attacks. When you start making biblical stands that really mean something, somebody, on the wrong side of the Bible, really gets upset. And he throws anything and everything he can get his hands on at you.

Sometimes, I can laugh at him and say, "Thanks for letting me know I'm on the right track." Other times it's a little harder to get through. Especially, when he attacks my family or uses them to attack me.

And so, the journey continues. We are anxiously awaiting and seeking for what the Lord has for us next.

www.ingramcontent.com/pod-product-compliance
Lightning Source LLC
LaVergne TN
LVHW010548160826
845677LV00013B/3045
* 9 7 9 8 9 8 5 4 1 6 7 5 6 *